Joan Callaway

"I wrote a review of a book on parenting for my last newsletter and almost before the ink had dried, one of my readers told me about another book - *Life in the Family Zoo* - which I found to be excellent — perhaps even a little more concrete. The author believes chore charts and family meetings are essential. I agreed with so much that the author wrote — no wonder I liked the book.'

Sherry Lohman - Child care provider and parent

"Using the ideas in your book help me dramatically change a difficult relationship with my daughter. My husband has even read the book and we are starting family meetings this week. I gave it as a gift to the parents of children I care for."

San Francisco policeman

"This class is the best Criminal Justice offering I've taken in 20 years as a street cop. I have a better understanding of working with people in the streets as a result of taking the class and reading the book *Life in the Family Zoo* — a great book!"

Book review by Maurice Bullard for *Oregon Individual Psychology Newsletter*

"There are many good things about this book. Platt knows Dreikurs!! He not only accurately converts principles into practices, he knows the intent of Dreikurs. The reader is not left trying to find ways to use the principles. While hitting hard in presenting Dreikurs, he does not use wording which arouses hostility, a most desirable trait as an introductory book. The wealth of examples is most useful; it could be called, 'A Do It Yourself Book.'"

Marie Colorado, Mother of three, grandmother of two

"I really enjoyed the whole book, but I especially enjoyed the chapter on encouragement and how it differs from praise. This is definitely the most important part of positive parenting."

Helen Childers - grandmother of six

"I wish I would have had this book when I was raising my four children. I enjoyed the book and the ideas so much that I think I might have four more to see how it works (just kidding, of course). I have sent *Life in the Family Zoo* to all my children."

Life
in the
Family
Zoo

By John M. Platt, Ed.D

Published by:
Dynamic Training and Seminars, Inc.
Publishing Division
Roseville, California

Second Edition

Library of Congress Catalog Card Number: 89-86019

ISBN: -0-9624446-1-8

Published by:

DYNAMIC TRAINING AND SEMINARS, INC.
PUBLISHING DIVISION
8902 Quartzite Circle
Roseville, CA 95661

Editors: Gail Golomb, Roseville, California and Gertrude Platt
Book design and typography: Graphic Masters, Roseville, California

TABLE OF CONTENTS

A Human Being's Strongest Desire is to Belong • Chores and Setting up a Chore Chart • Special Time with Children

All People Have Equal Claims to Dignity and Respect • Autocratic Parenting Style—Order Without Freedom • Anarchy-Permissive Parenting Style—"I, Me and My Freedom Without Order" • Democratic Parenting Style—Limited Freedom and Limited Choices • The Definition of a Mother • Example of Anarchy-Permissive Style • Example of Democratic Parenting Style • Limited Choices

Family Constellation is not an Excuse for the Child's Misbehavior • The Oldest Child • The Second Child and/or One who becomes the Middle Child • The Youngest • The Second of Two • The Only Child • All Our Children • Looking at a Problem in the Family Wholistically

FOREWORD

This book fills a gap in the literature devoted to parent education and adult/child relationships. So many available books are either an insult to the intelligence of the reader or written solely to enhance the academic standing of the author. John Platt has overcome both of these difficulties by producing an intelligent book which is a practical guide to child rearing and adult/child relationships at home and school.

One of the outstanding characteristics of Dr. Platt's work over the years has been his ability to distill the practical aspects of the method of improving the quality of adult/child relationships developed by Alfred Adler and refined by Rudolf Dreikurs. Dr. Platt's years of experience have provided him with many delightful examples of real situations that are extremely helpful in instructing parents and teachers to understand the underlying theoretical considerations of Adler's teachings.

Adler developed a philosophical understanding of the nature of man which held that the highest form of human interaction was based upon the ideal of equality. Dreikurs further developed the concept by formulating guidelines for creating a democratic family based upon the awareness of the equal worth of each member. Leadership in a democratic setting, either the classroom or the family, requires that the leader understand human behavior. How to motivate appropriate instructive behavior is the charge each parent or teacher must accept as part of the job. The concepts of purposive behavior, and methods of influencing children's behaviors are part of this book. The reality of winning the cooperation of children and an awareness of the need of children to feel a sense of belonging as basic to developing a positive self-concept, are dealt with in some detail.

By encouraging cooperation among children, rather than competition, each child in a family or classroom is allowed to attain the fullness of personal development. As parents are taught to use logical consequences rather than punishment to teach their offspring the rights and wrongs of social living, the need for children to rebel, seek power or revenge is minimized.

Dr. Platt does an excellent job of presenting to parents and teachers alternatives to traditional autocratic methods of discipline and affords many concrete ideas for assisting parents in becoming a match for their children. Of particular note is the encouraging theme of his suggestions to parents which shows the ultimate respect for both parent and child. He suggests a variety of adult behaviors that parents can implement to help children develop individual feelings of self-worth and a sense of belonging.

I am pleased and proud to have been invited to provide a Foreword to this work. I am confident that anyone, teacher or parent, who reads this work and makes an effort to put the ideas and suggestions into effect will realize amazing changes in their relationship with their children.

Oscar C. Christensen, D.Ed.
August 1989
Internationally-known Adlerian Counselor
Full Professor at University of Arizona

INTRODUCTION

I have often thought about writing a book on parenting, but the excuse I have used for not completing this task is because I believed "it had all been written before."

However, after being in the counseling field for 25 years, I have realized that there are always different ways to say the same things and different techniques for implementing specific ideas.

This book is full of specific techniques that help families develop a cooperative, respectful atmosphere in the home. These techniques are based on some really solid foundational beliefs.

In the past, there have been many approaches to human relationships (especially for parents and teachers) that have come and gone. Some were around for ten, even fifteen years, then all of a sudden, one does not hear about them anymore. I call those "pop psych." People learn new vocabularies to show that they really are "in touch" with "what is happening" in this "new approach" to understanding ourselves and others.

Adler's and Dreikurs' ideas have been around for centuries (as discussed in this book's first two chapters). Every recommendation that I make as a counselor to myself or to others is built on some of these basic tenets. They are not just techniques to make sure the other person does what I want him to do. Learning how to use choices to get more cooperation is one technique based on Adlerian principles of mutual respect and social equality.

When one studies Adler's and Dreikurs' ideas in depth, it becomes obvious that the philosophy, and even the techniques are more "eastern" than "western." Martial arts are an example. Persons trained in one of the martial arts do not try to overpower the opponents only with power. They use the power of the opponent to "throw him." They move with the "energy" of the opponent. That is what Adler and Dreikurs taught about dealing with power-oriented people. You dissipate power by disengaging in it.

Dreikurs would often say, "We no longer take the wind out of the sail; we need to learn to take the sail out of the wind." When the wind of power is blowing we must take the sail away and learn to solve our problems by working together rather than trying to subdue the other person (opponent).

Parents are often told to show their children more love. I definitely believe that love is an important emotion in positive relationships. My problem with those who say we should love our children and each other more is, "What do they mean?" Webster's definition of love "to hold dear: cherish," is probably not enough for all of us. When we talk about developing and enhancing a more positive, mutually respectful relationship, we can talk about some specific techniques that will help. What is love for one person might not be the way another person would describe it. Many times, parents' "love" for their children can be manifested in overindulgence, or overprotection (by not letting children experience the consequences of their choices or behavior), or wanting the children, as well as ourselves, to be perfect.

So, in talking with people about, "How do we love each other?" I try to shift to ways we can practice mutual respect and develop a more cooperative atmosphere in the home. Feelings of love or closeness grow when we are helping and cooperating with each other.

This same feeling is reduced when we are competing or fighting with each other.

Clients in a counseling session often say, "We really had a good weekend!" When I ask, "Well, what did you do?" (expecting them to tell me that they had gone to San Francisco or Lake Tahoe) they may reply, "We worked in the garden together," or "We got the wood stacked in the garage," or "We had a great time putting some photo albums together."

Working together to encourage each other and our children to become the responsible, productive, helpful, happy kind of people that we want them to be is specifically what this book is about and why I wrote it.

Striving for perfection is rampant in our society today. We all have to look perfect, act perfect, smell perfect and be perfect. It's not possible! The purpose of this book is to help parents enhance family relationships, not make them perfect. An editing friend of mine, who was reading the manuscript before this book went to press said, "I wish I had known these ideas before. I have made so many mistakes. We were not brought up this way." She felt discouraged after reading the book.

This is not why I wrote the book. If you become discouraged, give the book away or sell it at a garage sale. We can't do anything about what happened in the past but we can learn from our mistakes to do something about the present to influence the future.

The book is divided into six chapters—Belonging, Equality, Family Constellation, Four Goals, Logical Consequences and Encouragement. Within each chapter are mini-sections which describe specific ideas and techniques for dealing with certain kinds of behavior that we are confronted with on a daily basis. I have learned some of these techniques from others. Many are a result of being a father for nearly 30 years and working actively with parents for 25 years. This book is definitely not a book of "psycho babble."

Dedication

To my Mom and Dad—they taught me a lot about family living. And to Ann, my wife, for her love, support and encouragement over the last 31 years.

THE DESIRE TO BELONG 1

A human being's strongest motivation is to belong.
Our children's feelings of security or insecurity are directly
influenced by the feelings of belonging they have in the family.

The first class I took on Adler's and Dreikurs' philosophy about understanding human beings was from Dr. Ray Lowe at the University of Oregon. The ideas were simple and understandable. For years I had tried to understand Sigmund "Fraud's" ideas on the Oedipus complex, penis envy, and different fixations. I was not only unimpressed, but I was angry when I tried to figure out how I would handle a student in my high school classroom who had one of these maladies.

I would often ask my college psychology professor, "What do you do with someone who has penis envy or the Oedipus complex?" He would respond, "We'll discuss that when we talk about individual differences." I either missed that class or we never did discuss it.

I had to take Dr. Lowe's class. It was required of Oregon teachers in order to maintain their credentials. I found it enlightening to hear that both Adler and Dreikurs suggested that human beings are *social beings* and that their main needs are to belong (to contribute and to feel needed), and to feel competent within the family, school and, ultimately, in society. These are major cornerstones of their philosophy. Adler talked of *social interest.* He believed we are born with the potential to develop self-interest or social interest. If we allow the child to grow up believing that he does belong and has a place in the family, the school, and eventually the community, the child can be more "other-oriented" than "self-oriented." Adler believed that the more social interest a person has, the more mentally healthy he is, and conversely, the more self-interest he has, the more mentally unhealthy that person is.

After hearing Dr. Ray Lowe talk about social interest, I tried to figure out a way that I could implement this idea in my classroom. I thought of a student of mine who had been at the high school for almost seven years. He was 21 years old, almost as big as I was, and he definitely had better control of the classroom than I had.

I knew this the moment he walked into my classroom, dropped his books from six feet up, and had everyone's attention. He always did this shortly after I had taken roll and gotten the class under control. I wondered, how can I "need" this person? I decided I would ask him to take roll for me. I called him into my office after class one day and asked him if he would do this. I was really surprised that he was willing to help me out.

I explained to him that I was in trouble with the principal because I didn't pull the window blinds down correctly in the front of the room, and I didn't take roll right, and that he could probably help me out. When John Jones heard that I was in trouble with the principal, he could appreciate that because he was always in trouble with him. Thus, he agreed to take roll for me. From then on, he got to class a few seconds before the bell rang, grabbed the roll book, and sat in the back of the room to carry out his new job.

I noticed that all the students were now coming to class on time. I heard him say from the back of the room, "You better get your rear ends in here or I'll kick 'em." I tried not to listen to this, but I realized that he had much better control over the class than I had. As time went on, we became fairly good friends; we respected each other more. He still got an 'F-' in the class because he never handed in any assignments, but our relationship was entirely different.

I finally learned the reason he had stayed in high school for seven years was because he was the first of his "clan" to graduate from 8th grade, and now there was a chance that he could graduate from high school. His grandmother had left him a trust fund in her will which stated that as long as he stayed in school he would get $200 a month. Her hope was that he would go on to a junior college, or a four-year university, but not stay in the same high school until he got on social security. However, he was a very clever kid and had figured this out. He was way ahead of the game. Even in this situation, as bankrupt as I was with this person, just needing him to do something gave him some feeling of making a contribution or of having real power.

I often ask parents, "When your two year old-child comes up to help you, and he really wants to help, what do you say?"

The replies I often hear include, "Leave me alone," and "Don't bother me now." The classic one of, "You can help me when you're bigger" evokes the following response: "But, Mommy, I'm big enough now."

Most parents will reply, "No, you're not big yet, not until you're 12 or 14 years old. Now go play in the backyard, or go play in the traffic, or go swimming."

The child might answer, "I can't swim, Mommy."

A frustrated Mommy will answer, "Try it anyway!"

The message to the child is that, "If you want to help me or make a contribution to my life, leave me alone!" This is a modern approach to *needing* our children.

Here we have the two year-old going out into the back yard to swim or just stay out of Mommy's way. He says to himself, "I am really helpful to my Mommy when I leave her alone or when I become nonexistent." This obviously is not helping the child develop a very high degree of belonging or self-esteem.

When the boy is eight years old, Mother reads an article in *Parade Magazine* suggesting that children should have responsibilities in the home. She talks with her husband. He agrees that this is a good idea so they call in their son who has been running around the back yard now for six years. "O.K., Johnny, things are changed around here and you're going to help," they tell him.

"No way, Mommy," says Johnny. "I wanted to help when I was two and I have trained you to be my slave! I have no interest in helping out now!"

At this time, it is very difficult to get some kind of cooperation from Johnny. However, Mommy says, "You are still going to have a job" and the first job most children get is take out the garbage.

Now, Johnny says to himself, "I was really helpful to my Mommy when I didn't exist. I stayed out of her way, but now I really feel good about myself because I get to move up to garbage!"

I say all of this facetiously, but for me this is one of the biggest issues regarding our children today. The fact is that we could do very well without them. Children are appendages, a possession that gives us joy, but they don't make any contributions. However, we need to change this around with chores in the home, with tutoring programs in the school, and by offering children the opportunity to make some kind of contribution to the welfare of the community.

It's amazing to look at the statistics from 1930 to 1960. In that period of time, we changed from 70% rural to 70% urban. This gives us an idea of where children have been in regard to contributing to our society. In the rural farm setting, children were absolutely necessary. You couldn't do without them. People had large families just to survive. Eight year-olds drove tractors; three and four year-olds brought in the wood, gathered eggs, carried water and were consistently making some kind of contribution.

Today, I constantly hear people say that parents don't spend enough time with their children. I believe this is true, but I don't think that is the issue. In the 1930s and 1940s, how much time did Mom and Dad spend with their 12 children on the farm each night? In fact, they probably felt lucky just to know the children's names. However, the major difference between that period and today is that those kids grew up knowing that they were needed and that their contributions were important to the family's survival.

The average age of a Pony Express rider in 1849 was 16.2 years. There were 13, 14, and 15 year-old, pimply-faced adolescents riding across the country doing the most dangerous job in the United States at that time.

Nowadays, if there is mist in the air, children have a difficult time getting to school without a ride from someone. There is major grid lock near almost every secondary school in the nation because these students may get their Reeboks dirty or wet, or their Vuarnet glasses may get misty, or their hair may go straight or curly (depending on what is in or out of style). We have indulged children to the point that we have been very discouraging to them. We somehow believe that if we buy them transformers at age three, transistors at age eight and TransAms at age sixteen, our children are going to be happy. Obviously, this is not the case and while many people agree that we should not indulge or overprotect our children, we continue to shower them with toys. We unknowingly create an atmosphere where children are not needed and where they don't belong.

We are all concerned about rise of gang activity in our communities. I believe the growth in gang populations has happened because the gang offers children a chance to belong even if it is on the useless side of life.

Because this need is so strong, people will do almost anything to "have a place" or to belong.

Chores and Setting Up a Chore Chart

If there is any proof to Adler's and Dreikurs' premise that human beings are social beings and they want to belong, all we need to do is watch young children when we "let" them help. The contented look they get on their faces is obvious. Our 16 month-old granddaughter was watching the adults clean up our family room after some remodeling construction. Before we knew it, she had a rag and was doing what the other human beings were doing, which was scrubbing the floor. She did this for almost thirty minutes. She continues to enjoy helping by carrying dishes to the sink where a parent is waiting to put them in soapy water.

We need to set up chores on a developmental basis for really young children. There was a mother in one of my parenting classes who announced to the group that her two year-old daughter Stephanie, could set and clear the table. Of course, everyone was very skeptical. She explained that the family of six all passed their plastic dishes down to the end of the table where they were placed on a plastic chair. Stephanie would waddle back and forth to the kitchen carrying the dirty dishes. A dish pan of soapy water was on a low stool by the sink. She would put the dishes and silverware in the pan and head back to get more. (This would not be the way an eight year-old or 13 year-old would clean the table).

Mother then explained how Stephanie could also "set" the table. Mother would put each place setting on a low stool in the kitchen. The girl would carry the place settings into the dining room and place them on the chairs around the table. When the rest of the family came to dinner, they picked up their plates from their chairs, put them on the table, and sat down to eat. Emily Post probably wouldn't approve of a table set in this manner, but this mother was more concerned about the child developing a sense of belonging and competency, rather than what others might think. In these two instances the little girl was doing jobs usually reserved for someone much older and she felt good about it. Mother would often comment to other adults, when Stephanie "wasn't listening" on how helpful her daughter was by setting and clearing the table. Stephanie beamed.

Setting up a Chore Chart

I suggest to parents, when setting up a Chore Chart, that *ideally* all members of the family be included in daily jobs that keep the family functioning. This demonstrates a real commitment for cooperation within the whole family.

A list of daily chores can be drawn up by the parents, or by parents and children together, depending on the age of the children. The Chore Chart idea has been used for years but the following chart is one I have developed over the years. The first column on the Chore Chart would list the chores that need to be done on a daily basis. There should be enough chores listed so that when the number of people in the family is divided into the number of chores, an even number comes out. For example, if there are five people in the family there would be 10, 15, 20, or 25 chores. The following is an example Chore Chart for a family of four:

The Chore Chart

Chore:

Feed dog

Get newspaper

Scoop dog droppings

Set table (Evening)

Help with dinner (open cans, etc.)

Make salad

Clear table (Evening)

Sweep kitchen floor

Now that we have the chores listed in the left-hand column of the Chore Chart, I suggest that all names of family members be written on a small piece of paper and put into a coffee can, hat or some other small container. Drawing out names to see who gets what job takes Mom and Dad out of being the ogres who gave the most difficult job to the most difficult child. If you get accused of favoritism after the drawing, all you have to say is "talk to the can, or hat." (This technique can be used to determine who sits in the car's front window seat, and the order of children doing special things like taking turns on the swings, or riding a bike).

I learned this technique from a mother who came to talk to me about her four stepchildren whom she had just inherited as a result of a recent marriage. She had never been married before and had had very little contact with children. The children's first mother, who had been a "Super Mom" and did everything for the children, had died in an auto accident a few years previously. A "nanny" was hired to take care of the four boys, ages 15, 13, 11 and 9, and she also did all the chores around the home. The stepmother knew she did not want to be a "slave" to these four "brats," so I suggested she go home and set up a Chore Chart. She did and at the following meeting she told me what happened.

First, she made up the chores and told who was to do what. The older boys complained because she favored the younger ones and gave them the easier jobs. So she said (secondly), "O.K., you guys make up your own Chore Chart." After hours of arguing, they had a Chore Chart and now the younger boys said, "It's not fair; the big guys do all the easy jobs and left us with the hard ones." So Stepmom said (thirdly), "O.K., you guys, write down the chores, put your names on little pieces of paper and put them in this hat." As they drew their names out of the hat, she put them next to the chore in that order. When they still complained about how unfair it was, all she said was, "Talk to the hat!!"

Now we have two columns of the Chore Chart completed. What the chores are and who does them.

Chore	"Who Does It"
Feed dog	Dad
Get newspaper	Pat
Scoop dog do	Chris
Set table (Evening)	Pat
Help with dinner	Chris
Make salad	Mom
Clear table (Evening)	Mom
Sweep kitchen floor	Dad

The third column can be one of the most important parts of the Chore Chart because it sets a time limit for chore completion. In the above Chore Chart, Dad could be given the choice of feeding the dog (see Chapter 2 on Limited Choices) as soon as he gets up or before he comes to breakfast. He might ask Chris, "Do you want to scoop up the dog droppings as soon as you get home from school or before dinner?" and "Pat, would you like to set the table ten minutes or five minutes before we eat?" These choices are now listed in the third column of the now completed Chore Chart.

Chore	"Who Does It"		When It Will Be Done .
Feed dog	Dad	-	As soon as I get up
Get newspaper	Pat	-	Before I take morning shower
Scoop dog do	Chris	-	Before I come to dinner
Set table (Evening)	Pat	-	5 minutes before we eat
Help with dinner	Chris	-	30 minutes before dinner
Make salad	Mom	-	15 minutes before dinner
Clear table (Evening)	Mom	-	As soon as dinner is over
Sweep kitchen floor	Dad	-	As soon as dish crew is done

I have found it very helpful to have the third column "When It Will Be Done," when the Chore Chart is first instituted. When the parent says, "Chris, the Chore Chart says it is time to help with dinner," Chris is more inclined to do it than when the parent says, "It's time to help with dinner, Chris." Children respond better to inanimate objects, whistles, bells, hand clapping, and lights dimmed than to adult voices giving orders.

After a week, two weeks, or a month the chores can be rotated or another drawing can take place. This would be an agenda item for a family meeting to make plans. It is **important** to have some in-or pre-service training for each job that is unfamiliar to the child.

Special Time

For the busy parent, setting aside "Special Time" for a child is sometimes difficult, but it is very important in giving children a sense of belonging.

I have always appreciated both the Fram Oil filter ad which reads, "Pay me now or pay me later," and the old White Owl cigar ad which reads, "One way or the other, we're going to get you." Children, by their behavior sometimes make similar demands on their parents. The message is, "Either you spend some special time with me, Mom or Dad, doing something enjoyable together, or letting me help, or I will drive you nuts in order to get you to notice me. One way or the other I'm going to be recognized."

This is one of the reasons why I suggest setting up "Special Time"with children on a day-to-day basis. Often when both parents work outside the home they are so exhausted when they return that all they want is to be left alone. That is why it is important to set up a "Special Time for Chris and Pat." This might be Dad spending ten minutes with Chris while Mom spends ten minutes with Pat. After ten minutes, they exchange children or the children exchange parents. During this time, parent and child could do some activity the child wants to do. This doesn't have to be anything spectacular. It may be playing a board game that could be stored under the bed, talking about "our day," playing catch for ten minutes, or reading together.

While this needs to be done consistently, it may not be possible to do it every day because of other scheduled events which may interfere. The planning of "Special Time" could be an agenda item for the family meeting. I have found that what happens when parents set up "Special Time" with their children is that at first, parents and children alike both enjoy this activity. As time passes, and things are going pretty well, some families "forget" or put off "Special Time." It seems we don't forget how to get angry, blame, criticize or put down. I hear many parents who never forget to say, "Here I come home from work. I am so exhausted and none of you kids have done any chores. I'm sick of all this!!" However, we can forget about following through on "Special Time" and doing encouraging activities.

Additionally, letting the child know how much you appreciate this time together through a letter of encouragement (see Chapter 6 on Encouragement) is helpful. I am convinced that the quality of the time spent together is more important than the quantity.

Questions

1) According to Adler and Dreikurs, what is the main need of all human beings? p. 1

2) Why is it important for a child to develop social interests? p. 2

3) What do we tell most two year-olds when they want to help? p. 3

4) What are some of the major differences between raising children today vs. 50 to 60 years ago in a more agrarian society? p. 4

5) What are the author's three main steps for setting up a chore chart? pp. 6-7-8-9

6) Why do we need to set up a special time with our children? p. 10

2 THE CHALLENGE: EQUALITY OF WORTH

"People, Despite All Their Differences and Abilities Have Equal Claims to Dignity and Respect"
— Rudolf Dreikurs

Equality is Adler's second important concept upon which his philosophy is based. His idea regarding the *equality of worth* was talked about in the early 1900s. You can imagine how well accepted this idea was in pre-fascist Europe.

When I talk with parents and teacher groups about equality, I try to stress that equality does not mean sameness. That's how we see it too often. Many people believe that if we say children are our social equals, then they have the same privileges, responsibilities, knowledge, and social experiences. That is not the case. Children, however, as human beings have equal worth. Dreikurs' definition of equality is simply stated: "All people, despite all of their differences and abilities have equal claims to dignity and respect."

Adler taught us that all human beings, regardless of size, sex and race, have the same worth as every other human being. Just because someone is a doctor doesn't mean he's better than someone who isn't a doctor. People think that that sounds great, but when it comes to reality, that's not how it happens. Living with each other in an egalitarian relationship is very difficult. One of the reasons is due to the fact that we have no tradition for treating each other as social equals. The following chart is a concise definition of what will be discussed in this chapter.

Autocratic - Order without Freedom -
Parent Stance: "Do what I say because I say so."
No choice

Anarchic - (Permissive) Freedom Without Order -
Parent Stance: "What do you want? I'm here to serve your every need."
Open Choice

Democratic - Order with Limited Freedom -
Parent Stance: "Do you want to feed the dog now or before dinner?"
Limited Choices

Autocratic Parenting Style

The autocratic model, that most of my generation knew, was order without freedom. You were told to do something, and if you didn't do it, there was some kind of immediate punishment. That was permitted because people accepted the idea that they were worth less than someone else. Women were worth less than men. Blacks were worth less than whites. Children were worth less than adults. It was an orderly society. Most people didn't like it, but there wasn't much social change until after World War II.

At that time, men came home from the war and found "Rosie the Riveter." When Dad went off to war, Rosie (known previously as

"Mom") went off to work to support the kids. She raised the family and found she could do it. When her husband came home from the war, he announced, "O.K., Honey, that's all over. Get in the back of the bus because now I'm taking over."

What did Mom say? She said, "Oh, no, that time is all gone." As soon as that happened, the whole autocratic structure began to fall apart. It all began to crumble.

Dreikurs suggested that when the husband lost control of the wife, they both lost control of the children because the whole system broke down. If the wife didn't have to follow orders, then the response from the kids was, "Why do *we* have to do it?"

Anarchy-Permissive Parenting Style

Soon, a whole group of sociologists, social workers and educators came along and told us we shouldn't raise children in autocratic homes and schools if we want children to grow up surviving in a democratic society. Most people said, "That's a great idea. How do we do it?" The authorities replied, "Well, we don't know; we just think it's a great idea."

What followed was that we went from an autocratic family/ school structure right through a democratic approach, and ended up with anarchy/permissiveness. We went from the autocratic concept of telling children to "Sit down and shut up. Do what you're told!" to "Well, what do you want to do today, sweetheart?"

"Well, I'd like to write the 'F' word on the walls," the little sweetheart would say.

"O.K., here are felt-tip and grease pens; now go express your own identity," Dad would say. It was/is chaos in many homes and schools.

That set the tone for the 1960s and 1970s. We had encounter groups where people were getting in touch with themselves and their feelings, even to the point at which some left their homes and families to "find themselves." Some felt no responsibility to anybody except to "me." It was the opposite of the autocratic family structure. The common words were "I, me, and my"—not "we, us and our." It was freedom without order, and probably even more destructive because there were no limits. When you try to set up limits in an anarchical (permissive) family, the children say, "Forget you. You don't set any limits for me because I do whatever I want and it's not fair if you do."

In a classroom years ago, I overheard a teacher talking to a little "kindergarten anarchist." Mrs. Batiste said in a calm voice, "Joey, you cannot throw chairs in the classroom. Susie is now in intensive care at Methodist Hospital because yesterday you threw a chair and hit her in the head."

"Well, Susie should have moved her head," replied Joey. That's the way people in a permissive system think. *Anarchy* is a great system for a *society of one.*

If you listen to convicts talking, their conversations follow this same anarchical thought process. They believe "The only reason I'm 'doing time' is because I got caught."

If you ask, "Are you a criminal?" the answer is, "No, I just got caught. It wasn't my fault."

I have a tape-recorded interview between a minimum-security prison warden in Wyoming, and an inmate of that institution. The warden asked why the inmate was incarcerated. The inmate replied, "I was convicted of aggravated assault, but I didn't do it. The guy ran into my knife." The warden laughed at this ridiculous thinking, but the inmate didn't because he really believed what he was saying.

Then the warden asked, "He ran into your knife three times? Backed up and ran in, backed up and ran in, backed up and ran in?" The convict's thinking was that he wouldn't have stabbed the person if the victim hadn't been there.

A wave of permissiveness has swept this country. Looking back, we realize it was a scary time and only now are we probably seeing some of the results of this earlier thinking.

Democratic Parenting Style

The democratic parenting/teaching style that I am presenting is based on order with limited freedom and limited choices. In a democratic society we have freedom of choice to do anything we want to do. However, the choice to do whatever one wants takes freedom from others.

It is our responsibility as parents and educators to train children to be aware that we have choices, but in order to live cooperatively and responsibly in a democratic society, we have to accept the fact that there are limits. I can't drive on the wrong side of the freeway, but I can drive on the right side, with the radio on or off, the windows up or down, and between 50 m.p.h. and 70 m.p.h. I have some limited choices but not open choices.

If we analyze these three basic systems, that is, autocratic, anarchic permissive, and democratic, we realize we don't have much choice if we are going to live with each other in some kind of cooperative, peaceful relationship. If we are going to use the autocratic structure, then we have to get some people within either the family or society to accept second class citizenship. In order for me to be "the boss" (the autocrat) I just have to get Ann (my wife) to accept that she is less than I am. If I can accomplish that (Ho, Ho; He, He; what a joke) then the autocratic system "will work"and there will be some order in the family.

It seems logical to me that this is not going to happen. Therefore, we *must* learn to live with each other as social equals, and in an atmosphere where responsibilities are shared, and problems are solved through mutual respect.

Definition of a Mother

Now, let's look at how a normal "good" mother might function during the morning breakfast routine using the autocratic, anarchic/ permissive and democratic parenting styles. Before I explain this, I would like to give you my definition of a mother so I won't be accused of being a sexist. My definition of a mother is *"the adult in the family best trained by the children."*

This definition became a reality in 1971 when we lived in the San Fernando Valley where I was teaching at California State University at Northridge. I had a great job, but it was a terrible place to live. Ann and I grew up in the Midwest (Iowa and Nebraska) and had lived in Oregon, and Tucson, Arizona. For us, the San Fernando Valley was culture shock at its greatest. We just couldn't figure it out. We lived there 11 months, 3 weeks, 2 days, 1 hour and 12 minutes. We were desperate to get out of the smog-filled valley.

Finally, when a family counseling position became available in Northern California in the Elk Grove School District, I made an immediate airline reservation, flew up, interviewed, and got hired. I returned home and told the family (Ann; Gordon, 10; Jeff, 8; and David, 5) that I got the job and we were "getting out." Everyone was happy—to say the least! Ann volunteered to sell the house. I said, "Great, we'll save the money we would pay a realtor, and instead use it as a down payment on a home in Elk Grove."

We obviously didn't know what it was like to sell a house on our own. We thought we'd just get a little 'For Sale' sign, hang it on a tree, and somebody would come by and write out a check. We thought we'd put our furniture in the U-Haul, and we'd be gone. Well, it didn't work that way.

First of all, we decided to move after the famous 1971 earthquake that shook the valley. Real estate was not really selling too well. However, after many problems, Ann finally got the house sold. She came home from closing the deal really upset. She kind of threw the contract at me and said, "If you want to sell houses, you sell them!!" I really didn't ask her to sell the house in the first place, so I couldn't figure out why she was so upset with me. My mother and father, who lived in Santa Barbara, came by our home on their way to the Sierra Mountains. I suggested maybe Ann would like to go with them for a short visit as a little break. She took the suggestion, a few clothes and was gone. There I was alone with our three sons.

I can remember thinking to myself, "I'll put this theoretical stuff into everyday practice and show Ann how this parenting goes." We had a calendar on the refrigerator in the kitchen. After the first day, I marked out that day on the calendar. I was pretty proud of myself for having made it through that first day. I did notice a little dryness in the right side of my throat, but I thought it was from smog, or sinus problems.

On the second day, I made another mark through that day on the calendar and I noticed that both sides of my throat were dry and one eye had started to twitch involuntarily. By the third day I found myself, at noon, marking off the morning.

The fourth day began as I marked off the hours, 8:00 to 9:00 a.m., 9:00 to 10:00 a.m., and 10:00 to 11:00 a.m., I could hear myself saying, "Now, where the hell is she? A woman's place is in the home. Children need their mother."

Finally, on the fifth day, she came home. She walked up to me, and I had a little pinafore apron on and my hair was greasy and kind of hanging down in my eyes. She said, "Honey, it looks like you're glad to see me."

I replied in a faltering voice, "How the hell could you tell?"

About five minutes later she was lying on the couch, laughing hysterically.

I went over to her and asked her, with my eye involuntarily twitching, "What's so funny?"

She looked at me and said, "Honey, it's you. It's the funniest thing I've ever seen. You sound like me, you look like me and I'll bet you even smell like me."

I had been running around yelling, "I told you kids to get this crap picked up out of the family room! Get your hands washed! Get to supper, now! Stop this incessant fighting! After all, Lord knows what I've done for you kids, and this is the thanks I get." That was when I realized motherhood had nothing to do with reproduction. It had more to do with who is around the children the most and, thus, gets best trained by them.

Now let's look at the three child management styles as demonstrated in a breakfast scene.

Example of Autocratic Parenting Style

In the autocratic situation, when Nathan (age three and one-half) comes to breakfast, Mother knows best. Autocratic people know everything there is to know about everything. They love to be right. They have lectures to go along with all of the things they "know." While everyone hates to listen to the lectures, autocratic people have them readily available. Finally, Nathan sits down and Mother says, "There's no choice. This morning you're having white gruel." White gruel is another name for Cream of Wheat. You pour it out of the pan and it goes "flop," lies in the bowl, and shivers. Nathan says, "But Mommy, I don't like white gruel." So Mom starts a four-step procedure to try to get Nathan to eat the "gruel."

In Step 1, she says, "You need it. It's going to be much colder today; I can already feel it in my knees. Boy, do they ache, and you need this to stick to your ribs."

So the three and one-half year old takes Mother's advice literally and in his mind he is trying to figure out, "How will this stuff stick to my ribs and protect my knees?" He knows that Mother's a little strange, but he takes a few bites and says, "Mommy, it's still yucky and I don't like how it tastes."

Now comes Step 2. "We'll fix it," Mother says. "We'll put molasses, wheat germ, brown sugar or raisins in it to make it better." She then takes a couple of bites to demonstrate that you can eat this "yuck" without disintegrating. She doesn't like it any better than he, so she tongues it and puts it in a plant. He doesn't see her do this; he figures if Mother can eat the white gruel, he can eat it. So he takes a couple more bites and Mother can already feel that if she gets up a half-hour early to make this hot cereal for this little cherub he's going to eat it. "I'm sick and tired of him not doing what he's told," she thinks.

However, "the cherub" is sitting there saying to himself, "Boy, I'm not going to eat this yuck; I hate it." But Mother doesn't want to have a big confrontation like she did on Monday morning. So Mother starts the next stage, Step 3. I call it the "Sociologist's Lecture."

The "Sociologist's Lecture" is her last humanistic effort to get Nathan to eat the gruel. It starts off with Nathan asking, "Mommy, why do I have to eat this gruel?"

"Because somewhere in Bangladesh the children are starving," says Mother patiently.

Now Nathan says to himself, "I have no idea where this place is but I'll eat for the kids over there." He takes a couple of bites, stops and thinks, "This doesn't make any sense. Why do I have to eat it for them? They're the ones who are starving."

Mother is now in the middle of a power struggle. Nathan, who has been doing a lot of thinking, says in a whiny voice, "I don't want to eat this yucky stuff. Why do I have to?"

Mother finally loses control and says, "Because I said so!!"

"I'm not going to eat it and you can't make me," says an angry Nathan.

Now she's had it. "Listen, little cherub, I've had it with you." She gives him three good swats on his rear end and says, "You go out in the backyard and I'll see you at lunch time."

Nathan runs outside crying, "I don't love you any more. All the other kids get to eat Hoopity Doopty Sugar Scoops and I have to eat this white gruel. You're the worst mother I've ever had!"

When he's finally out of the house, Mother starts feeling really proud of herself because she stood firm and she let Nathan know who runs the show in the house. This feeling goes on for 10 or 15 minutes, but of course, she's a "Good Mother," and like all Good Mothers, she starts to feel guilty.

Her thoughts center on the fact that she sent him out in the backyard with nothing to eat. It said in that psychology book never to take food away from children, or hit them so hard. Why, her hand is still sore. After about 10 or 15 minutes of building up enough "guilt power," Nathan comes back into the house and walks up to Mother. She's standing there with her arms crossed. She's got one last lecture. This one is the funniest lecture of all for parents to give.

In Step 4, a tearful Nathan says, "Mommy, Mommy, I'm so hungry and you sent me away from the table."

Mother lovingly looks at him and says, "If you would have done what your mother said, you wouldn't be in this mess." She doesn't usually stop there; she goes on and on with "The Endless Lecture."

When she finishes that lecture, she gives him three graham crackers, a Hershey Bar, and an orange and he runs out to play. "I'll see you at lunch time when we will have brussel sprouts and liver to make up for the nutrition you missed at breakfast," she yells after him.

Guess what lunch is like? Once the "I Told You So Lecture," also known as "The Endless Lecture-Part 2" begins, the child will get a "the lights are on but nobody's home" look. He hears very little of this "wonderful lecture."

I was interviewing a 15 year-old boy many years ago. I asked if he listened to his mother when she was yelling at him. He replied, "I hear her, but I don't listen." That was one of the first times I thought about the semantic difference between "hearing" and "listening."

Two important aspects of the autocratic style of parenting demand that the responsibility is on the boss/parent and that there is no choice for the child.

Example of Anarchy (Permissive) Parenting Style

Now let's look at the Parent/Mom who is raising a little anarchist for a future revolution. Rather than for mother to order the child to eat "white gruel" she goes to the other extreme and offers an open choice.

"What would you like for breakfast, darling? I am here to serve your every need; I have no rights as a human being. I'm only a mother. If you would like, go get the kids in the neighborhood, and your brothers and sisters and come trod on me; I'll be lying here on the kitchen floor," she says. This is the complete opposite of the autocratic.

Johnny responds by demanding his eggs over-easy, a minute steak and a piece of French toast. Mother tells Johnny to go into the television room, get dressed and she will prepare his breakfast. She works frantically in the kitchen preparing the requested feast, getting the table set, putting vitamins in the spoon and lighting the candelabra. Johnny's dressing process has stopped and with about three minutes before the car pool arrives to take "darling" to preschool, Mom turns into a "Huey Helicopter Mother." She races around, speaking at a very high rate of speed, "Get out here, Johnny, you have to have breakfast, the car pool will be here in three minutes, you haven't brushed your teeth, combed your hair, taken your vitamins," etc. etc.

At this point, she is trying to jam his arms into his shirt and the car pool pulls up. The driver honks three times and then leaves because they are tired of waiting for Johnny every morning. So guess what Mother does? Does she drive him to preschool so he won't miss out on his early education? No! She drives him because she doesn't want to spend the morning with him.

These two aspects of the anarchy/permissive parenting model illustrate how the responsibility is still on the parent, and still the child has open choices which are disrespectful of both Mom and the child.

Example of the Democratic Parenting Style (Stance)

Now we come to the scenario where the parent is using the democratic parenting style to give the child a sense of belonging. When Keith comes to breakfast in this setting, he has responsibilities to help get breakfast ready. He puts the spoons or forks on the table, and he gets the cereal out. He makes a contribution to the welfare of the family and develops a sense of belonging.

Then Mother gives him a limited choice. (See section on Limited Choices page 23.).

"Would you like your fried eggs easy-over or sunny-side-up?" she asks.

Keith may respond, "But Mommy, you know I don't like fried eggs. I prefer mine done Huevos Ranchero style."

At this point, Mother might say, "If you don't want the fried eggs, then we will see you at lunch." Keith probably will get a somewhat puzzled look on his face and respond, "Oh well, I'll take mine over-easy." Or maybe today is cereal day. Mother will ask, "Do you want Wheaties or Cheerios?"

Keith says, "I want Wheaties because I want to be just like Michael Jordan and Mary Lou Retten."

So Mom gives him Wheaties; he puts milk on the Wheaties and begins to eat them. All of a sudden Keith says, "Those people that advertise Wheaties are liars. These Wheaties are really yucky."

At this point, all Mother has to say is, "I'm sorry but you made the choice. Either you eat the Wheaties or we'll see you at lunch."

An astounded Keith replies, "But that's not fair, Mommy."

His response can be very much like the child in autocratic

scenario, tearfully crying, "I don't love you anymore. All the other kids get to eat Hoopity Doopty Sugar Scoops." All Mother has to say, in a very friendly tone is, "I'm sorry. I'll see you at lunch. We will have peanut butter sandwiches and a glass of milk."

With tongue in cheek I assure parents that their little darlings will make it to lunch-time because scientists did research at the University of Oregon and found out children can go 21 days without food.

In this situation, respect for both parties is maintained and the child learns to make choices and live with the consequences.

The eating process in many families has become a source of a great deal of conflict. If we would handle the activity more matter-of-factly, we probably wouldn't have some of the eating disorders that we now have. As an example, I always ask parent groups how many people who are anorexic (will not eat) or bulimic (gorge and vomit) come from low-income families? They know the answer: very few.

In a low-income family, if at the dinner table one child said in a whiny voice, "Momma, I don't like these beans," one of his brothers or sisters, with a loud inhaling sound would consume those beans in a hurry. At the next meal, the whiner probably wouldn't say anything about the beans because they are better than what he had at his last meal: nothing.

Helping children to make choices and to learn to live with their decisions is important to the development of the child as a responsible, happy, contributing human being. The rest of the book will be dealing with these two basic concepts—first, helping children develop a sense of belonging (and of feeling competent) and second, creating a democratic atmosphere where cooperation and being responsible are the main goals.

Limited Choices

Limited choices are helpful in getting cooperation from others. The autocratic parenting style (referred to earlier) was based on orders and disrespect. Ordering children around is ineffective in developing a cooperative family atmosphere. When we order power-drunk people to do something, they resist either passively or actively.

Imagine Mom saying to her son, "Joey, go feed the dog!"

"Why do I always have to feed the dog? Sally never has to; I have to do everything around here!" whines power-drunk Joey.

"Joey, I said feed the dog, NOW! I mean it—if you don't start taking care of the dog, we are going to give it away," yells Mom.

"Oh, you won't give the dog away; you love him more than I do," Joey says with a sly grin.

Finally Mom, completely exasperated, spanks Joey, and sends him to his room. She feeds the dog herself.

In the *laissez faire* permissive parenting style (anarchy), Mom asks sweetly and pleadingly, "Will you please feed the dog, darling?" Susie says, "I'll feed him later." Later never comes, so Mom feeds the dog.

The parent using a democratic style would use limited choices. My opinion is that this is our *only* choice in dealing more effectively with our children. The autocratic system is almost totally ineffective and even if it "works," it helps to create a power-oriented relationship between adult and child. As I mentioned before, anarchy is a great system for a society of one. If there is only one person in the social system, he can do whatever he wants. If there is more than one person, a choice must be made between the autocratic or democratic.

I believe *all* children need choices. Over the years I have suggested the use of limited choices to parents of power-drunk children. Eight years ago, I did a workshop for street police from Los Angeles and San Francisco. One of the participants, a beat cop from Market Street in San Francisco, came up to me after the workshop and said, "I am remarried; my wife has two children and I have two, and I see how choices might be helpful in dealing more effectively with them but how could a cop use choices on the streets?"

I told him quite honestly, "I have no idea how one would do that." We went our separate ways and three weeks later he called me from San Francisco. "I have to tell you what is going on, John. It's the funniest thing in the world and I can't believe it. I never arrest anybody now unless I give them a choice," he said.

"How in the world do you do that?" I asked.

"I ask them 'Do you want to be handcuffed in the front or behind your back?' They stand there like little puppy dogs and hold their hands out in front. My partner and I do not have to wrestle them to the ground and it makes life so much easier. It may be against regulations, but we don't have to fight with them any more and that's nice. We never tell them to get into the car. We always ask, 'Do you want to get in the right side of the car or the left?' and they walk off like real tough guys and get into the car."

Then he ended our discussion of choices by saying to me, "If the drunk on Market Street deserves the dignity of a choice, don't our kids?" This is when I decided *all* children need choices.

There are many important things that happen when we use limited choices. The use of choices is not just a trick to get children to do what we think they should.

1.) It is a demonstration of *respect*. No one wants to take orders any more.

2.) If the child is into power and resists every order, giving him a choice may *change his power-like thinking*. Rather than the child saying, "I'm not going to do that" it might be, "Do I want to do it now or in five minutes?"

3.) People always ask me, "If we use choices, will it always work?" I facetiously respond, "If it always worked do you think I'd be sitting here talking to you? I'd have my own Lear jet and I'd fly all over the world telling people to just use choices; your children will all go to college, be responsible citizens and never touch drugs."

All I really can say is that we are talking about *probability*. There is a higher *probability* that you will get cooperation if you use choices than if you order or beg the child to help out.

4.) When the child says, "I will feed the dog in five minutes," he has made a *verbal contract* with the parent. Now, the parent can remain friendly when monitoring the child's behavior. This is a very important result of using choices.

5.) Using words like *"later"* and *"after"* are not limited choices. I call "later" and "after" words of eternity. "Later" and "after" never come. If you ask, "Do you want to take out the garbage now or later?" and the child responds, "I'll do it later" you've set yourself up for a problem. You may very well say, "O.K., dear, it's later now so take out the garbage." Of course the child will respond, "It may be later in your book but it's not later enough in mine."

We need to use words like "before" or "as soon as." When using limited choices ask the child, "Do you want to take out the garbage now or before dinner?" or "Now, or as soon as the TV program is over?" When setting up a choice, keep place and time in mind. Offer the child a choice by saying, "Either you can stay in the family room and play quietly or you can run and roughhouse in the garage or the backyard," or "Do you want to set the table now or ten minutes before dinner?"

6.) Choices can be used for almost any kind of behavior. The only time choices should not be used is in a dangerous situation, or if you are in the middle of a power or revenge cycle with the child. You can imagine asking, "Do you want to get out of the way of the oncoming Mac truck now or in five minutes?" We must act without talking when in a dangerous situation.

7.) There is an interesting and very important part of using limited choices that many people do not consider. If we want to have an orderly atmosphere in the home where the parent is in control, we need to *share* power. Those who are afraid to share power (teachers, administrators, parents, bosses, etc.) often lose control. Sharing power with children through family meetings, class meetings or by giving choices, gives children the feeling of power in a constructive and useful way. If we don't share power with them, children struggle to gain it (usually in a useless way) and demonstrate to adults that they are not in control.

It is a paradox. The person who wants to have control loses control of himself very rapidly when it looks as if he is not in control of others. I try to help the person with a controlling personality use this characteristic as a *plus*; being in control of oneself helps one to be in control of the *situation* but not necessarily in control of others.

The following is an example of using limited choices which

would include all of the above facets. Dad could say, "Sally, your dog Rover needs to be fed. Do you want to feed him now or before dinner?" (Dad shows respect by using limiting words like "now" or "before" and he is also sharing power.)

"Oh, I guess I'll do it before dinner," Sally replies. Her thinking changes with a higher probability of Dad gaining cooperation, and she has made a verbal contract.

Dinner is put on the table and Rover still has not been fed. Sally comes to the dinner table with the rest of the family and now all Dad has to say is, "Sally, you need to feed Rover (friendly reminder). Should I put your food in the oven or leave it on the table while you take care of the pup?" (another choice).

If the child says neither choice is acceptable, I suggest to parents that they just repeat the same choice a couple more times. If there is still no cooperation, the choice then becomes "How long do you need to be in your room to decide which choice is acceptable, five or ten minutes?"

If the child says, "I will never make a choice. I'll rot in hell before you can make me do it. I hate the whole world!" I would suggest withdrawing from that kind of confrontation. (More on this when we talk about power struggles later on in the book.)

Here is an example list of possible choices that one might utilize to increase cooperation:

1. Do you want to take a shower or a bath?
2. Do you want to draw your water for the bath or do you want me to?
3. Will you need 30 or 45 minutes to do your homework?
4. Do you want to do your homework as soon as we get home from school/child care or 30 minutes before dinner?
5. Do you want to clean your room as soon as you get up in the morning or before you come to breakfast?
6. Would you like to work on the even-numbered problems first or the odd-numbered ones?
7. Do you want to brush your teeth with warm water or cold water, with your left hand or your right hand, or as soon as you put on

the toothpaste or I do?

8. Would you like to set the table or make the salad?
9. Do you want to wear your blue sweater or the yellow sweater?
10. Do you need to get up at 7:00 a.m., or 7:10 a.m. in order to be ready for breakfast at 7:30 a.m.?
11. The football game is over at about 10:30 p.m. Do you want to go get a snack with your friends and be home by 11:30 p.m. or at midnight?
12. Do you want to change your clothes now or before you eat the lasagne?
13. Would you like to take your nap now or as as soon as we read the sailboat book?
14. Would you like to hold my hand or have me hold your hand?
15. Would you like to clean your room by yourself or would you like to help me clean my room and then we'll clean yours together?
16. Do you want to walk through the house or go outside to run?
17. Do you want to tutor on Monday, Wednesday and Friday at 10:00 a.m. or on Tuesday and Thursday?
18. Would you like to start your warm-up activity as soon as you get in your seats or as soon as the tardy bell rings?
19. Do you want to pay $2.00 or $2.50 out of your weekly allowance for the $26 broken window?
20. Do you want to get booked first or change into prison clothing first? (Youth counselors who are orienting California Youth Authority wards to a correctional facility).

Many times, when I meet parents they will say, "John, I remember you gave a talk many years ago at Kennedy Elementary School and you talked about limited choices. Just that one technique has made it so much easier to carry out my role as a responsible parent."

Using limited choices can make life much more pleasant. Try it; you may find out how helpful it can be.

Questions

1) What is Dreikurs' definition of equality? p. 12

2) Many people make an important mistake in interpretation of equality. What is this? p. 12

3) Why is living with each other as social equals so difficult? p. 13

4) What are the parental stances in the autocratic, democratic and anarchical parenting styles? p. 13

5) According to the author, when did atmospheres in families really start to change? And why? p. 13

6) Why did we go from the autocratic to the anarchical, or permissive style of parenting? p. 14

7) What are the common pronouns in the permissive family atmosphere? p. 14

8) Why is it so difficult to live with someone who grew up in a permissive family atmosphere? p. 15

9) According to the author, what must we teach ourselves and our children? p. 16

10) What is the author's definition of a mother? p. 16

11) Why did he come up with this definition? pp. 16 - 17

12) What four steps does the autocratic mother go through to get the child to eat "white gruel"? pp. 19 - 20

13) What two important mistakes are we making when we use the autocratic style of parenting? p. 21

14) What does the "Huey Helicopter" mother do? pp. 21 - 22

15) What two important mistakes are we making when we use the permissive style of parenting? p. 22

16) In the democratic family system, what is the first thing a child might do in preparation for breakfast? p. 22

17) Why do very few people with eating disorders come from low income families? p. 23

18) What choices did the street policeman give people he was going to arrest and what important lesson did the author learn from this man? pp. 24 - 25

19) What is the second most important aspect of giving a child a choice? p. 25

20) Do choices always work? p. 25

21) What words do you specifically want to leave out of a limited choice? And what words are helpful? pp. 25 - 26

22) Why does the author believe that parents and teachers are losing control of home and school situations? p. 26

23) After reading the author's examples of limited choices, list three that would be helpful in your home/school situation. pp. 27 - 28

FAMILY CONSTELLATION:IT'S NOT WRITTEN IN THE STARS 3

Family constellation offers an understanding and possible explanation of the way a child sees life, but not an excuse for the child's misbehavior.

Adler developed many of his ideas from reading literature. He noticed in reading novels and plays about families that brothers and sisters in the same families often were very different. He also began to realize that children in the families he counseled were likewise very different. One important contribution he made to understanding human beings is the information he provided in his description of Family Constellation or Birth Order.

As one studies this idea, it becomes very logical how one's position in the family *influences* (but does not determine) one's outlook on life. The characteristics that I describe later in this chapter are not absolutes; they are only based on probability. It is *probable* that an oldest child, or a middle child, will have certain characteristics.

No two children are born into the same family. My older brother was born into a family that had been husband and wife and after his birth became Mom and Dad (an interesting experience for everyone). I was born into a family where there already was a "kid," so in some respects "it's no big deal" when the next one comes along.

It is interesting to look at the baby books of our children. The oldest child's book is in perfect order—every new happening is documented, locks of hair are in cellophane bags and perfectly glued into the book. The second child probably has a book, but most of the pictures are stuffed in for permanent gluing at a later date. The third child doesn't even have a book.

Many things change as more children are born into the family. The parents can become more relaxed. After all, their first child should be at least a Stanford University graduate with a little advanced work at Oxford. As parents begin to realize some of their expectations are a little unrealistic, they tend not to get so upset when the younger children aren't so perfect. Finances change and money is not such a big problem, or the opposite is true; it costs so much to raise children today. Also, today many families are single-parent or blended.

No matter what changes happen, the most important element is not so much what happens to the children, but how they see or interpret what happens. Children are great observers but they often are lousy interpreters.

The older child (sometimes referred to as the "dethroned" child) observes that when his younger sibling comes into the world some dramatic changes take place. The younger child cries, fills its pants, vomits, and can get a tremendous amount of attention. "My parents spend so much time with the baby" is an accurate observation by the older child but the interpretation that, "They must love him more" is faulty.

We wonder why the older child often "reverts" to baby behaviors—talking baby talk, soiling his pants or whining. It is logical when you look at it from the older child's point of view. "If that little guy can get all this attention for doing those baby things, why shouldn't I?" he asks.

Many times we have looked at little children only as reactors to their environment or as products of their hereditary genes. We must look at children as active persons who influence the environment and decide what to do with their hereditary endowment. When you take one child out of the family, everything changes; each member of the family has such an influence on the atmosphere of the family.

Dreikurs talked about Adlerian psychology as a "Psychology of Use." It's not so much what we are born with (hereditary endowment) but what we decide to do with it. How many parents of a gifted child are frustrated because he doesn't live up to his potential?

No matter how many children are in the family, there are only five positions—the oldest, the younger of two, the baby of three, the only child and the middle child. A family of 10 or 12 children has groups of three, two or an only child. This is somewhat affected by age splits and sex differences.

The question the child is always asking, consciously or unconsciously, is, "How do I fit in; how do I *belong* in this family?" If the older child has some areas already reserved for high performance, the second-born will often take the opposite tack. Because of the competition in the family, the first two children tend to be the most different. "I can't compete in his area so I'll pick out another where I can be successful," says the second-born. The fewer children (down to one) in the family, the more competitive they are for Mom and Dad's recognition.

The Oldest Child

The oldest child wants to maintain a position of superiority over the second. He may do this by always wanting to be first—getting up first, getting through the door first, or getting work done first. Years ago, I worked with a family where the oldest son (nine years old) always got a headache when he ate ice cream with his two younger brothers (seven years old, and five years old). In order to finish first, he would inhale the ice cream and then reach for his head and say, "Oh, my gosh that hurts." It was more important to be number one than to be free of headaches.

Older children tend to be bossy and critical. They love to criticize their younger siblings. The younger ones "enjoy" getting criticized because the older one gets into trouble for being *so* critical of his brothers or sisters. When our oldest son was 13 years old, he asked me why I criticized him for criticizing his younger brothers. I had no answer. That's kind of like hitting the child for hitting his siblings. We are beating up on the older one while we are saying, "There will be no violence in this family!!"

People who are critical of others are usually critical of themselves. People who are constantly finding fault with others are not usually very encouraged themselves. "If I'm not too sure how good I am, at least I have to show you how you are worse."

One of the real tragedies about our society is that so many of us think we have to be perfect. Perfectionism is a **curse**. Every one of us knows that it is impossible to be perfect, but we want to be perfect anyway.

The one who usually has the highest degree of perfectionism is the oldest child. "If I'm perfect, no one can catch up with me or be better than I am," he believes. "To be human is to be perfect" is often their outlook on life. Obviously, this can lead to a great deal of discouragement and frustration. It is a heavy burden to always try to be perfect. It is important to note that trying to do the job as perfectly as possible is not the issue.

The issue really is, "If it doesn't turn out as perfectly as I want, then I am a failure." So, with the oldest child, we need to be aware of this perfectionism and do what we can to reduce the stress that it contributes to one's life. Attempting to encourage the discouraged, perfectionistic, oldest child often becomes a difficult task. Allowing ourselves to make mistakes without putting ourselves down can model a healthy attitude. Encouraging the "deed" rather than the "doer" is helpful (see chapter on Encouragement).

Sometimes we get 'overconcerned' about our oldest's "over-concern." I find it helpful to give the perfectionist the right to be perfect. We might say to the child, "I don't think always having to be perfect is going to help you be very happy, but if that is your decision I can't do much to change it." Encouraging the child to feel that "I'm okay just the way I am; I don't always have to be perfect or better than others," would also be a healthy outlook to help all our children develop.

Oldest children tend to be the responsible ones. They get a lot of recognition for being responsible which many times is manifested in their being overprotective of the younger children.

Orderliness is very important to the oldest. "Everything has a place and everything should be in its place." To be in control is really important to the oldest. That's why they are so vulnerable to their younger siblings. All you have to do is show the oldest that they are not in control. Just a little sickening smile can set the oldest *off.*

The oldest child loves to compete in sports, as long as he wins. However, he worries so much about winning that this often gets in his way. Being the oldest is a pretty tough position.

The Second Child and/or One Who Becomes the Middle Child

The second child comes along and looks at the older one and says, "Boy, that guy works so hard to be perfect, I guess I'll be the opposite." The second-born tends to be the opposite of the first.

I describe the second-borns as "affable slobs." They know that if they get up in the morning and look out the window and don't see the sun, it will come up another day. If it doesn't come up that day, it will be up sometime—don't sweat it—whereas, the first-born has a stop watch and log to make sure the sun comes up when it's "supposed to." He'll go so far as to report it to the proper authorities if it doesn't come up when it's supposed to.

Sometimes, the second-born acts as though he is in a race by always moving. Some refer to the second-born as a steam engine or the "little engine that could." If the oldest child gets discouraged by the second one's success or for other reasons, he may give up and the second-born sibling sometimes takes over the role of being first. Dr. Christensen of the University of Arizona labeled this child the *Avis* child. They are second, but they try harder.

If the second becomes the middle child, he often becomes the "Social Worker." Seconds have a strong feeling for the underdog. The oldest child gets all the responsibility and the baby gets away with murder. "Lord knows I try," is often the cry of the middle one. Middle children have been referred to as the "squeeze child." The attitude that "life is not fair" is often the outlook of the middle one and pouting is often a common behavior.

When I do workshops with parents, I put them in groups by position in the family and then ask them to discuss what they liked and what they didn't like about their position. In the 15 years I have done this, the middle-child group has always put down as a negative "hand-me-down-clothes." The middle child always got "hand-me-downs" from the first-born and then the baby got new clothes because the middle one wore out the "hand-me-downs." It's no wonder middle guys get the feeling of being left out.

The Youngest

Along comes the third or the youngest child in the family of three children. He is the charmer, the manipulator, or the service seeker. The youngest is really good at getting others to do things for him. Whereas the oldest child is the bossy one, the youngest is the boss. The oldest child tells everyone what to do and no one does it. The youngest child doesn't tell anyone to do it and it just gets done. "Me tie my shoes, I'm only 14 years old," might be the statement of the youngest.

The youngest have beautiful smiles and usually have long eyelashes. They are great actors/actresses but if their charm or manipulative techniques don't work, they often are the temper tantrum children. The youngest is usually the most spoiled child in the family. A common feeling of the youngest child is that he never really feels people take him seriously. He feels as if he is just taken for granted. No one really cares what he thinks.

For the youngest child to make a decision is sometimes difficult because someone has always made decisions for him. It is common for the youngest child to believe it is the teacher's job to teach but not the child's responsibility to learn. As a result he often has academic difficulties.

Since he is seldom given any responsibilities, he often finds it difficult to become responsible. The older one will do it "right" so the parents often go to the older ones when they want something done. As a result the youngest fails to learn about being responsible.

Their charm, attractiveness and ability to manipulate others can be real assets in their lives. We find the youngest child can be a good leader if our definition of a leader is someone who can get others to do things and delegate responsibilities.

The Second of Two

The second of two usually has characteristics of the middle and youngest children, except that they are not so pronounced. The more people the youngest has to train the better they get at it. The younger of two children only has three people to train (an older sibling and Mom and Dad), while the youngest of three has four people (two older siblings and Mom and Dad). One thing we can be pretty sure of is that the second child will be very different from the first sibling.

The Only Child

The only child is the special child in the family. He is often called spoiled, but I believe that spoiling is a result of comparing. The youngest is the spoiled one because in comparison to the older ones, he usually gets more and is often overprotected.

The only child develops the feeling of being special but not necessarily spoiled. He does have some of the responsibility characteristics of the oldest child. He definitely feels responsible for what goes on between Mom and Dad. The only child likes to have time by himself. He tends to be really good with people older and younger than himself, but he has difficulty with his peers. Oftentimes, peers see the only child as a 'snob' when in reality the only child who is eight years old doesn't understand why other eight-year olds are so "immature." The eight year-old only child is usually at about a 13-or 14-year maturity level.

The only child is often in competition with the same sex parent for the attention of the opposite-sex parent. The only-child male often competes with Dad for Mom's undivided attention while girls compete with Mom for Dad's attention.

All Our Children

There are pluses and minuses for any personality characteristics that we develop during the formative years. There is nothing wrong with being responsible. We need responsible people, but being responsible for everything and everybody doesn't work too well. It is helpful to be a manipulator when attempting to get people to work together. People can use their charm to encourage others. We all would want the typical perfectionistic oldest child doing open-heart surgery on us.

I try to help parents build on children's strengths rather than always trying to "cure" their weaknesses. Provide an opportunity for the oldest child to take responsibility in areas that are helpful in the home. Getting the family library or the toy box organized, making up a chore chart, or helping put some order into the garage would be helpful ways for the oldest to contribute.

We do not need to put any pressure on the oldest to perform. He does that very well himself. Sometimes the oldest gets so wrapped up in his own performance level that he is not concerned about helping others. I often suggest that we strongly encourage his contribution to others.

The middle child has a feel for the underdog so it's helpful to encourage him to assist his friends who are less fortunate. Try to utilize his problem-solving abilities in family meetings. Give the middle and youngest children equal responsibilities in the family. Don't have the oldest child doing everything.

Standing firm on completing the job is important with the youngest child. It may take him forever to get "it" done but even though it may be agonizing at the time, it is encouraging for him to see he can do it.

One could go on for chapters about the family constellation and there have been many books written about it (see Additional Reading). One of the most important ideas about family constellation is the influence it has on one's personality development. Many parents take too much responsibility for the difficulty their children may be having when a lot depends on how the children see themselves in the family.

Dreikurs suggested that the person who has the most influence on our personality development is not necessarily Mom and/or Dad but the sibling closest to us in the family constellation—the one with whom we are in most competition.

Understanding the family constellation can offer much information about how the child sees life. It is not a label or an excuse but an understanding or explanation. Our children will be different and that's O.K. They don't all have to be exactly alike or exactly what we want them to be.

Learning to accept children as they are, rather than what we think they should be, can be very encouraging. It says to the child, "You have worth as you are. You don't always have to live up to my expectation to be human."

Telling the discouraged oldest child who has a younger brother following him, "It must be tough to look over your shoulder and always see him there doing better," may give you immediate credibility with that child. Telling the second-born following a perfect oldest, "It must be difficult to always have to live in your sister's shadow." Being able to say "it" in the words of how the child thinks can give us tremendous rapport with our children. People often asked Dr. Dreikurs, "How do you develop rapport with your clients?"

"Show them you know something," he would reply. I believe this is true for parents, also.

We may do the best possible job we can, but we do not ultimately decide what kind of personalities the children have or what they are going to do with their lives. So *relax and enjoy!*

Looking at a Problem in the Family Wholistically

It is important to look at the difficulty we may be having with one child as a family problem or concern and not label the difficult child as the "identified patient." Many times the "good child" does all the right things for the wrong reasons which may be to make his sibling look like the "bad guy." We really can't understand the child's point of view unless we look at the total family situation.

For example, I remember a mother who called me years ago. She asked me if I would talk to her nine year-old son, Ryan, and "fix him." I jokingly said, "I am not a faith healer. I am a counselor."

I asked her if there were any other children in the family and, if so, it would also be important to bring them with her to see me. She told me she had two other children but they were doing fine, and she could not understand why I would want to see them, too.

I then asked her to give me the other children's names and ages, and to tell me a little bit about them. She started out with Elizabeth who was 11 years old. Her voice became much more calm. "She is very responsible and helps me out so much. She usually reports to me when Ryan 'flips off' the yard duty so I can punish him when he comes home from school. She basically is trustworthy, courteous, kind, cheerful, thrifty, brave, clean and reverent. That's Elizabeth. She was on the dean's list in preschool!"

Now you start to get an idea of how Ryan sees himself in the family.

"Who is the other child?" I asked.

"Well, there is Angela who is six, but we call her Angie," (it's common to put an *ie* or *y* at the end of the youngest child's name), "and she is absolutely the cutest kid around. She has long eyelashes, and she's definitely Daddy's favorite. She loves to sit on my lap 24-26 hours a day. She is not as responsible as Elizabeth, but she is so cute the way she gets out of her chores."

I then inquired about how Angie and Ryan got along. "Oh, they don't do too well together. Angie loves to go into Ryan's room," Mom said.

My tongue-in-cheek reply was, "Oh, really? I can't imagine she'd do that."

Mom went on to explain, "Yes, she loves to play with Ryan's model airplanes. She just kind of flies them around, but sometimes she drops them and then sometimes she mistakenly stumbles and steps on them."

I again replied, "What does Ryan do when Angie steps on his planes?"

"Well, he steps on Angie," she said.

I asked, "What do you do, Mom, when Ryan steps on Angie?"

"Well I, of course, step on Ryan," she replied. "He shouldn't be beating up on his little sister.

Now we have a pretty good picture of how Ryan sees this life. *It's not fair.* We can hear him saying, "I have an older sister who is perfect and who constantly loves to report when I'm bad, and a little sister who comes in my room and busts up my planes. If I do anything about it, I get in trouble. I try, but nothing seems to work out."

This information is not an excuse for Ryan's behavior, but it is helpful in understanding the situation and dealing more effectively with the family's concern. We would never really understand this situation if we looked at Ryan only as the "bad kid" who needs "fixing" and not look at the family from a wholistic point of view.

Questions

1) What does the author mean when he says "no two children are born into the same family"? pp. 31 - 32

2) What is meant by the statement, "Children are great observers but lousy interpreters"? p. 32

3) Why is the oldest child often described as the "dethroned child"? p. 32

4) What did Adler mean when he talked about a "Psychology of use"? p. 33

5) What five positions are there in the family? How can this be possible in a family of ten children? p. 33

6) Why is "perfectionism" such a discouraging trait? p. 34

7) What does Dr. Oscar Christensen mean when he describes the second-born as the "Avis child"? p. 35

8) Why does the middle child have a strong feeling of empathy for the "underdog"? pp. 35 - 36

9) Feeling "left out" is often the feeling of which child in the family? p. 36

10) Why does the youngest child sometimes find it difficult to make decisions? p. 36

11) Why is the youngest sometimes a very good leader? p. 37

12) What tends to be the most common characteristic of the only child? p. 37

13) How can the characteristic of being responsible have a plus and a minus? p. 38

14) According to Rudolf Dreikurs, who has the most influence on our personality development? p. 39

15) How can the "family constellation" information help adults develop rapport with their children? p. 39

16) Why is the "good" child so good sometimes? p. 39

4 FOUR GOALS OF MISTAKEN BEHAVIOR: A CRY TO BELONG

*"A discouraged child
is a misbehaving child."*
—Rudolf Dreikurs

udolf Dreikurs made a major contribution to the understanding of children's behavior when he developed the
concept of the four mistaken goals of discouraged and
misbehaving children. Previously, behavior had always
been described from a cause-and-effect point of view. It was believed
that the manner in which Father treated you would determine the way
you would behave. We now know that this is not necessarily true.

When we look for the mistaken goal of the behavior, we have
some techniques and options we can utilize to deal more effectively
with the child's misbehavior. *We can't do anything about what
happened in the past, but we can learn from our mistakes to do
something about the present to influence the future.* There is optimism in recognizing the four goals.

Dreikurs referred to children's misbehavior as mistaken—not
necessarily good or bad. The child's behavior demonstrated that "if
I can't belong in the family by being helpful or needed, then I'll find
other ways to be significant." While it is hard to change "bad"
behavior, a mistake can be erased overnight. Many times children

find it encouraging to know that they are not necessarily "bad," but that they have some mistaken ideas of how to be important. It is our job as adults to provide opportunities for children to become significant through their contributions and feelings of being needed and competent.

The chart on page 46, developed by Dr. Jerry Marquart and Frank Meder is very helpful in understanding the four goals. The antecedents and consequences that we can utilize as parents are listed in columns 7 and 8.

It is important to keep in mind that our first inclination in responding to the child's misbehavior is usually the most ineffective. If our children want attention (Goal 1), we give it. If they want to engage us in a power struggle (Goal 2), we usually fight with them. If they feel the need to be revengeful (Goal 3), we feel we have to hurt back. If the child has given up on himself or feels inadequate (Goal 4), we usually give up on him also.

The way to diagnose which goal the child is using is to examine how you feel during the interaction. (See column 4 on the chart). If you are feeling annoyed, it is usually attention that the child is seeking; if you feel threatened or provoked, the child's goal is power. If you feel hurt, the child's goal is revenge, and if you feel helpless, the child's goal is a display of inadequacy. Many times, Dreikurs' students would ask him, "Why do you put children who misbehave in these four categories?" He usually would respond, "I did not put them there. I found them there." A child can be using all four goals in different situations and with different adults.

Attention-Getting Goal

Of the four different behaviors, attention-getting behavior is dealt with most easily. Giving attention at appropriate times is helpful. When children play cooperatively together, we need to stop what we are doing and participate with them. "Can I join you two in playing school?" or "It's nice to see you enjoying each other," would be appropriate verbal responses.

← Discouraged child's movement if they lack the feeling of belonging →

COPING BEHAVIORS FOUND IN DISCOURAGED ADULT - CHILD RELATIONSHIPS by Jerry E. Marquart, Ed.D. & Franklin J. Meder, Sacramento, CA

Goal of all human beings is to belong

The four goals of misbehavior Column 1	Child's Action Column 2	What child is really saying with his/her behavior - Column 3	How adults often feel (e.g., teacher, parent) Column 4	Foreboding Typical Adult Responses Column 5	Child's Reaction to Adult's Behavior Column 6	Appropriate Procedures Antecedents Column 7	Appropriate Procedures Consequences Column 8
Goal 1 Attention (to keep others busy with him/her)	Pesters Nuisance Clowns Wants to be served Shows off	"I only count when" .. I am being noticed .. I am being served "I only count when" .. I do exactly what I'm told	Annoyed Bothered Irritated Wishing solitude	Coaxing Reminding often Complaining Whining	Temporarily stops disturbing behavior when given attention	Provide constructive attention at appropriate times Make "contracts" (When . . . then . . .) Follow through with	Determine who really "owns" the problem Ignore when attention is demanded
Goal 2 Power (seeks to be boss)	Apple Polishing" Perfect child. Compliance, Submitting, Conforming Buckling under	"I feel . . ." .. fearful.. uncertain .. uneasy.. anxious	Pleased Delighted Proud	Boasting, Doting Fussing over Gloating	Temporarily assumes a false sense of worth	Assist child in identifying alternatives, e.g., class meetings, family councils, etc.	Follow through with "contract" & apply logical consequences Avoid unconstructive attention (i.e.nagging)
	Resists doing what told Does opposite of what told Argues, lies, bossy, bullies, devious, sneaky, Temper tantrums Cheats, stubborn	"I only count when I .." .. win.. dominate .. do what I want .. am boss "I feel . . ." .. threatened .. provoked .. intimidated	Threatened Provoked Intimidated Thinks "He/she cannot do this to me!" Feels "I'm losing control"	Determined to control child's behavior Asserts "authority" (e.g.: orders child to room, to be quiet, etc.)	Continues behavior when reprimanded Feels has "won" when others get upset	Provide situations where child can use his/her "power" constructively Involve family/class in decision making	Give an "I" message Remove self from the area Enlist child's help Provide for cooling off period Use the agenda Active listening
Goal 3 Revenge (wants and tries to get even)	Defiant, Sullen Hostile, Retaliates Blames, Tattles Fights Kicks, bites, scratches, Calls names Vindictive Steals	"I only count when I." .. hurt others .. create pain .. get back at others "I feel . . ." .. angry.. bitter .. hurt.. hate .. I can't be liked	Deeply hurt Angry (extreme) Resentful Hatred Thinks "How could he/ she do this to me?"	Punishes Hits, slaps Verbally berates child "Banishes" the child (i.e.: overt/covert rejection)	Threatens (e.g.: "If you don't then I'll . . ." Intensifies actions (i.e., respect for both oneself and others) Hurts others Destroys property Runs away Delinquency	Display mutual respect Recognize conflict is inevitable, be willing to compromise Have the courage to be imperfect	Passive listening Acknowledging responses (e.g.: "Uh-huh." "I see." etc.) Avoid retaliation Do the unexpected
Goal 4 Display of Inadequacy (wants to be left alone)	Withdrawn Gives up easily An "isolate" Apathetic "Stupid" behavior Infantile behavior School phobias Compulsive eating Psychosomatic illnesses	"I only count when I ." .. don't bother others .. don't mess up .. don't try "I feel . . ." .. hopeless .. depressed .. inferior .. inadequate .. humiliated .. no good "I give up"	Extremely helpless Apprehensive Very discouraged Despair Quite tense	Throwing up hands Gives up Deny feelings Psychosomatic illnesses	Retreats or regresses further Becomes even more passive	Have faith in person's ability Trust person with small responsibilities Demonstrate behavior desired Emphasize successes Build on person's strengths	Using "door openers" Acknowledging responses Active listening Encourage child to try . . . minimize mistakes Don't expect immediate results

This chart is a composite from various sources; however, the ideas were primarily derived from the works of Rudolf Dreikurs, MD

Power Goal

In a power struggle the opponents often have to give up what they want in order to win. There is no winner in power or revenge.

How many children are either flunking out of school or performing only at a minimal level to show parents and/or teacher that "You can't make me do my homework, hand it in, or behave in class?" Ten-year-old Dusty came to me one day in early June and announced that he had defeated his teacher. I asked him how he had so successfully done this.

"I showed her, that horrible Miss Shark," (that is what he had nicknamed the teacher) "that she couldn't make me do my homework or do the work in class," he said joyfully.

"That's great, Dusty, you really used your power in a constructive way," I said. I then asked him what had happened as a result of his victory over his teacher.

He responded, "Well, I flunked fourth grade." Then he sat for a moment and the color in his face literally turned gray.

He looked at me and said, "Golly, Dr. Platt, it doesn't look like either of us won."

I agreed. "You hate Miss Shark, and she hates you. Now, you both have another year together and you have to go through fourth grade again," I said.

There are so many arguments that go nowhere except to escalate into hurtful feelings. Nothing is solved in an argument. There is no problem solving going on. How many times are these power scenarios being played out over and over again? We have to withdraw from these struggles and attempt to encourage cooperation in our homes (see section on Limited Choices for ways to deal with power).

Revenge

The goal of revenge is even more difficult to deal with because of the hurt the parent feels. I often talk with young children about revenge and I always ask them, "If I hurt you, what do you want to do to me?"

They almost always say, "I'll want to hurt you back!"

I draw a revenge circle on a piece of paper for the children. "Around we go. You hurt me and I hurt you. Around and around we go." Then I ask, "Who wins this battle?"

They almost always reply, "No one."

Isn't it amazing how aware children are that there is no winner in this situation, but that we keep on trying to win?

Another example of the revenge cycle happened a few years ago when a mother of a 16 year-old daughter called me at my home and told me she had just slapped her daughter's face 16 times because the daughter had called her a "bitch" 16 times.

She said, "I think we need counseling."

With tongue in cheek I suggested that her observation was quite perceptive.

The next day they came in to see me. I explained to the mother that the first thing she had to do was quit slapping her daughter's face. She informed me she would stop when her daughter stopped calling her names. I asked the mother, after our five minute counseling session, to go out in the reception area and send her daughter in to talk.

When the daughter came in, I explained what I had said to her mother and that her mother said she would quit slapping her daughter's face when she quit calling her names.

I no sooner got the words out of my mouth and the daughter said, "I'll quit calling her names when she quits slapping my face."

I called the mother back to my office and said to them both, "I recommend to you both to go home, call each other names and slap each other's face."

The mother began to cry and asked, "Are you a counselor?"

I told her that was my job description. She said, "Why would you tell us to do this?"

I replied that this is what they told me they were going to do.

The mother said, "Well, I can't stand this any more."

I said emphatically, "Well, then stop. Just stop hurting each other. Nothing can happen to improve your relationship until you take this first step."

That mother and daughter are not much different from the rest of us. We always want the other persons to stop doing what they are doing rather than looking at "what can I do in this situation?" When I look at what the other person can do to change, it is discouraging. When I look at what I can do to change the situation, it can be encouraging. It's optimistic. I can do something even if the other person won't do anything. It's much more productive when both decide to stop, but one person can do it.

Display of Inadequacy

The most difficult child to encourage is the child who is at Goal Level 4: display of inadequacy. He may not be inadequate, but he perceives himself as so. He has given up. Often this child won't try any more. He is so discouraged that he usually won't even try to do anything.

The only thing we can do is attempt to encourage any behavior that even appears to be an effort on the child's part. Sometimes catching him doing anything positive is helpful. Hand him a sack of groceries and say, "Thank you for your help. I couldn't have done it without you."

Children may not have given up in all areas. They may feel that they are completely inadequate in math or spelling, but feel they can be successful in a sport or in reading. I try to get the parents or teachers of these children to have them make a contribution to someone in their area of strength. Maybe they could tutor a younger child at school in soccer, or reading. Building on their one area of strength may give them the courage to try in other areas.

I worked with a teacher of handicapped children regarding a 15 year-old boy who not only had physical problems, but was completely discouraged. His handwriting was illegible. Every behavior modification technique had failed. Nothing seemed to motivate this child.

The teacher made a new plan as we discussed his complete discouragement. The first thing she did was to take down from around the room all of those black cards with perfect letters on them that have discouraged generations of young penmanship students for years.

Then any time the teacher could even get close to reading one letter on a page, she would circle it and put her initials beside it. She would then tell the student to cut out the letter and tape it to the top of his desk. Then when he was going to write the letter again on future papers, he could refer to his own example. It was amazing to watch him try harder. It took months, but before the school year was over, he could write in a legible fashion.

It is very important to understand what goal the child is pursuing because then the adult can determine what he can do to improve the relationship.

Our Priorities for Our Children Become Our Bug Buttons

It is important for parents to look at what priorities they have for their children. Is education most important to the parent, or that the children be happy, outgoing, compassionate or responsible? Treating the children fairly is a priority for many parents. Maybe we think that our children should treat their fellows with dignity and respect, or that they need to be nearly perfect in everything they do. Whatever our priorities are, children seem to figure them out and if they want to get to us, they zero in on our "bug button."

Since I was the middle child in my family, fairness has always been a priority for me because I *knew* I was never treated fairly. My brother got all the responsibilities and my sister got away with murder. I had a "Lord knows I've tried" attitude about life. If our three sons wanted to get me going, all they had to say was, "You're not fair, Daddy." I would definitely try to figure out how I could be more fair, or get into a long discussion about being fair. Neither method got anywhere.

As a high school teacher, I had two priorities for my students. One was to be absolutely fair, and the other was to try to provide an exciting classroom atmosphere where students would really want to learn. During the first three years of teaching all I ever heard from my students was, "You're not fair!" and "Your class is boring. It's really a drag, man!!" No matter what I did to be fair, I never was.

I would make up a test and read it to my wife. "Does that sound like a fair test to you, Dear?" I would ask.

"Turn the light off and go to sleep. It's 3:00 a.m." she would mumble.

The next day I would hand out my "fair test" and the students would complain, "You didn't talk about questions 13-14-15; it's not fair." I would tell them, "Just mark out questions 13-14-15; I guess I didn't talk about them." Having my students think I was not fair was really hard on me.

Finally, one of my students, Louie Bevanditch, came up to me and said, "You are going to go nuts trying to be fair! All the kids call you a 'fair freak.' All they have to do is tell you you're unfair, and you go off." As my eye twitched involuntarily, I asked Louie what he thought I should do. He told me to merely say, "I'm really sorry you think I'm unfair because I try not to be." And that's it; I started saying that to my students and they had no idea how to respond. It was as if they were thinking that somebody got to this guy and told him what was going on. Now, how are we going to bug him?

I kept thinking to myself, how can I respond when the students tell me how boring my class is?

One day when I was in the men's faculty lounge, Ed Oliver was the only other person there. Ed was about sixty years old, had a pock-marked complexion as a result of having smallpox as a child, and a short satanic-looking haircut. He wore the same sports coat for years, smoked cigarette butts out of the ashtray, and the students loved him!

I got up enough nerve to ask him, "Have your students ever told you that your class was 'boring'?"

"Well, John, sometimes at the beginning of the year they did, but not for long," he said, taking a cigarette butt out of the ashtray.

"What do you say when they tell you your class is boring?" I asked him.

He took a long drag on the cigarette butt and answered, "I tell them my class is a preparation-for-life-class, and life is a bore."

This is not what they told me in my teacher-training years. The professors in the Education Department always said, "Model enthusiasm because if you are enthusiastic, your students will also be enthusiastic." Many times the opposite is true. The more enthusiastic you become the less enthusiastic are your students.

In fact, the next day after my discussion with Ed Oliver I went into my class. The students were remarking how boring history is. They felt our society doesn't seem to learn from history because we do the same things over and over. I agreed with them saying, "I really didn't like history that much either and if I could get it out of the curriculum, I would. The only reason I teach the stuff is to make a buck."

A couple of the students responded, "Oh well, it's not that bad, Mr. Platt."

Recently, a family came to see me for counseling. At our first meeting only Mother and her nine year-old daughter, Katie, came. During the second meeting, Mother told me how bored Katie seemed to be. In fact, Mom was really worried that Katie was "depressed."

They had gone to Disneyland, and guess what? Katie was bored with Disneyland! When I talked with Katie, I suggested that she was the first nine year-old person I had ever met who was bored at Disneyland.

She informed me that it was "so hot" and that "we had to walk everywhere." As I talked with Katie and her mom, I became increasingly aware that somewhere in this family there was someone bursting with enthusiasm and who was a lover of life. Shortly, there was a knock on my office door. I opened it and in *bounced* the new stepdad who was recovering from drug and alcohol abuse, a born-again Christian and, according to him, someone who had a "love of life and others that is boundless."

As we talked, he told me about Katie. "She just infuriates me because she is bored all the time. There's more to life than being bored." It was obvious that his stepdaughter had found stepdad's priority on his "bug button."

Rather than get into an argument with children about some of these issues, I recommend diffusing the issue by using some of the following responses. This doesn't mean we can't talk about it later, but there's really not much sense in talking about it when someone is angry or hurt.

We can't change the way a child or any other person thinks, but we can change the way we react to that thinking. Most of the time children don't feel the way they say they do when they are angry. They just want their own way, or to see what kind of response they can get from the parent.

Child's Statement	Parental Response
"I don't love you anymore; I hate you."	I'm sorry you don't love me anymore because I still love you"
"I'm running away"	"I hope you don't because I would miss you a lot."
"You never let me do anything."	"I'm really sorry you don't think I let you do anything. Maybe we can talk about it when you are not so angry."
"You are the worst mother I have ever had." (Father has been married four times.)	"I'm really the worst of your four mothers?"
"You love Susie more than you love me"	"I wish you didn't feel that way."
"I'm so dumb."	"I'm sorry you think you're so dumb because I think you're a pretty smart guy."

When our boys would say, "You love my brother more than you love me," sometimes I would say facetiously, "You're right." Then they would invariably say, "Oh, you don't either."

The Homework Power Struggle

Since there has been a movement in the United States to "get back to the basics" in education, homework has, in some cases, seriously disrupted family life. The school system seems to go in cycles. For a while, there was no homework. Children got their work done in school. But now if children are to learn, many educators believe, we must have all children from kindergarten through12th grade **doing** homework.

It is nice for school personnel to tell parents, "Make your child do his homework." But if the child happens to be a little reluctant to study, the school system fails to inform parents just how they might get the homework done through cooperation.

Does the following family argument sound familiar to you?

Dad comes in from the garage and says to Ted, "Hey, Ted, have you done your homework yet?"

Ted continues to flip through a skateboard magazine while watching TV and mumbles, "I don't have any."

"What do you mean? You always have homework," says Dad.

"Oh, Dad," (whining) "I'll do it later after I finish watching Alf," says Ted.

"No, you won't. You'll do it now!" Dad angrily replies.

Ted is extremely upset, and shouts, "But, Dad, I want to watch the rest of Alf!"

Dad gives in a bit, settles down a little, and says, "O.K., you can do it after Alf is over."

Much later, Dad looks at Ted. "Did you do your homework?" he asks, now that Alf is over.

And, true to form, Ted says, "No, I'm too tired now."

However, Dad, completely fed up, replies, "I don't care how tired you are, young man! Get in there and do your homework now!"

The following system is not fail-safe, and does not always work, but the *probability* of getting homework done is higher if you use these ideas instead of fighting with the child. All that happens then is that the homework issue becomes a huge power struggle. Giving the child limited choices helps him feel in control.

The first choice (see chapter on Limited Choices) is to ask a child, "Do you want to begin your homework at 4:30 p.m., before dinner or at 7:00 p.m., right after dinner?" The second choice is to ask the child, "Do you need 45 minutes or an hour to do your homework?" The child answers, "after dinner for 45 minutes." The third choice is to ask, "Would you like to sit at the kitchen table or work in the family room at the desk?"

Now a plan for homework has been set up and the parent need not argue about it anymore with the child.

If homework was not assigned by the teacher, then the child can use the regular homework time for other learning activities such as reading an enjoyable book or doing math problems created by Mom or Dad or a sibling.

When parents establish a regular time and place, the nagging and eventual arguing about homework can be reduced dramatically. Children are more likely to remember to do their homework on their own if they have a consistent and regular homework time. The routine and structure helps improve a cooperative atmosphere.

It is my opinion that the parent's responsibility in the homework arena is (1) to help set up the homework time; (2) to provide a well-lighted area for doing homework; and (3) to be available for assisting the child but not for doing the homework. After the parent has done this, it is now up to the child to complete the homework.

As I mention in the Chapter Six "Communicating with Our Children," the first question (interrogation) we ask when the child comes home from school is, "Do you have any homework?" All the parent has to do with the limited choice system is to say, "It's 4:00 p.m. It's homework time."

It is important to find ways to encourage (see Chapter Six on Encouragement) children not only to complete homework, but to enjoy the accomplishment of learning. Help build the child's confidence by encouraging the effort he made. If the child has made some effort to do math problems, but there still are mistakes, a parent's response or comment could be, "It looks like you are beginning to understand your subtraction better" or "It looks like you got three more correct today."

Helping children *become* responsible is the parent's assignment but this does not mean *being* responsible for their children's assignments.

Lying Behavior

When the parents know the child is lying about something, I suggest a rule of thumb that is often helpful. That is, "Don't ask questions you know the answer to!" Lying is usually Goal 2, *power;* or Goal 3, *revenge.*

The reason it is so hard for parents to handle lying is because they often see this behavior as the child's first step towards becoming a criminal. If the child has not done his homework, than he can be considered irresponsible, but if he also lies about not doing it then this indeed becomes a moral issue. Having an irresponsible child is one thing, but having an immoral child is something much more serious. So, parents really are vulnerable to this kind of behavior. Usually parents who say, "I cannot stand anyone who lies," have children who tell "falsehoods."

Parents will often tell their children, "If you just tell me what you did and not lie about it, you won't get into trouble." The message children get from this statement is that "it's O.K. to misbehave as long as you don't lie about it." You can imagine a child who takes this one step further and says, "Yes, I did rob two banks and I shot a policeman as I made my getaway, but I didn't lie about it so it must be all right!" This, of course, is not the parent's intention.

The struggle starts as soon as the interrogation begins. A mother in one parenting group told me she caught her son taking cookies out of the cookie jar. When she asked him if he was taking cookies (interrogation) he replied, "No, Momma. I'm resting my hand" (on the cookie jar). Mom went into orbit. A more effective approach might have been to ask him how he would like to pay for the "borrowed" cookies—out of his savings or his allowance?

In another home down the street, Mom comes home from work. Pat is watching television. It is Pat's job to feed the dog. The dog is standing at the patio door with sunken cheeks and glazed eyes. Both his water and food dishes are dry.

Mom asks politely, "Dear, have you fed the dog?"

"Of course I've fed the dog," says Pat. Mom knows this is not true, flies off the handle, screams, and yells at Pat for lying to her again.

A more effective approach may be for Mom to walk in (knowing the dog has not been fed) and say, "Do you want to feed the dog now or as soon as the T.V. program you are watching is over?"

"But Mom, I've already fed the dog," whines Pat (attempting to bring Mom into the lying warfare).

Mom repeats the choice maybe even two or three more times until Pat gets up and gives the dog his "second" meal. However, the dog is now fed and the moral issue of lying is past.

A mother once called me to report that she and her 16 year-old daughter, Sally, had had a physical fight with black eyes, etc. As a result, Sally had run away from home. Later, she was brought home by the police and now Mom wanted a counseling appointment with me so her daughter "can be fixed."

When they came to me later that day, I first spoke with Mother. She told me that they had had difficulties for a long time, but it was Sally's incessant lying about *"everything"* that was really destroying their relationship.

I asked Mother for an example of Sally's lying. Mother explained that she was somewhat of a health fanatic. She ran marathons, and ate bark, seaweed, and other delectable items. Every time she was going to make a health food specialty, the main ingredient was gone. The explosion that lead to this fight happened as a result of Sally taking Mother's sunflower seeds (the main ingredient), eating all of them and lying to Mother about it. The evidence was overwhelming. There were sunflower shells and an empty package on Sally's bedroom floor.

Mother approached Sally and demanded, "Did you take my

sunflower seeds, Sally?"

"No, I didn't," answered Sally. "You always accuse me of everything around here."

"I can't believe it! There you go again lying to me, you little witch!" said Mother angrily. The fight began. All of this was confirmed in my discussion with Sally.

I spoke to Mother about my "rule of thumb;" that is, that a parent doesn't ask questions to which she already knows the answer. We role-played and practiced saying the correct words.

A week later, they both came back to see me and Mother was really excited to report the successful use of "the rule of thumb." Mother was ready to make a special dish using carob-covered raisins. Once again, the main ingredient was missing. Mother went down the hall, and after practicing the choices she would offer her daughter, said to Sally, "Do you want to go to the store now and buy another package of carob-covered raisins or as soon as it stops raining?"

Mother Nature was on Mother's side because shortly after the choice was given, the rain stopped and Mother heard the front door slam. Thirty minutes later Sally returned, threw the package on the kitchen counter, and said rather rudely, "I didn't steal your stupid carobs!"

Mother replied very firmly and kindly, "Thank you for replacing them." That was the end of it. She didn't scream, yell and get in a physical fight with her daughter, but she did stand firm and the outcome was so much more productive when Mother used the "rule of thumb" regarding lying.

If money is missing from Mom's purse and Chris is the only one at home besides the dog, rather than asking Chris if he took the money, ask him how he wants to pay it back. "Do you want to give me the $5.00 now or shall I take $2.50 plus interest out of your allowance for two weeks?" This strategy can get a parent out of many struggles over, "are you lying to me again?"

If the children have lied in the past, parents will often test them to see if they are still lying. For example, if the parent goes by the child's room, and the room looks like a disaster, the parent knows in a split second that the room has not been cleaned. If the parent asks the child, "Have you cleaned your room?" the struggle begins again.

Parents always ask me, "How will children know the difference between right and wrong, lying or not lying, if we don't tell and lecture them about it?" The problem is not that they don't know the difference, but getting them to do what needs to be done. Many parents have found this way of dealing with lying behavior is very helpful.

Giving the Child Permission to Misbehave

Sometimes when we give power-oriented children permission to do what they are not supposed to do in a safe, structured setting the behavior ceases. Giving permission takes the power out of the situation and reduces the excitement of violating a rule. The following are a few examples of this approach:

Match Lighting

Fire is intriguing to many of us. We like to sit in front of the fireplace for long periods of time watching the flames. Children today seem to be even more intrigued by fire and by lighting matches. When a child has actually started a fire or come dangerously close to lighting one, the parents might take the child to the local firehouse to see and hear from the firemen about the consequences of match lighting in dangerous places. Firemen usually have a display of, or at least pictures of, what fire can do — kill, maim, destroy, etc. Some children respond by thinking, "Wow! I'm never going to light another match." Yet other children often times think, "Wow! Look what I can do with matches!"

I suggest that parents do what my mother did with me.

When I was five, I probably could have been labeled a pyromaniac. I loved to light matches and I did this with my friend from next door. My mother realized I was into the match-lighting phase of my "social development" and decided she needed to do something about it. She didn't accuse me or yell at me. She just asked me to light every match that needed lighting for about a two-week period.

I could be across the street at the park playing with my friends, and Mom would call me home to light the cigarette for Mrs. Jones. During those days we burned trash, and lit the gas stove, oven, and the broiler so we used matches a lot more than we do today. No matter what the situation, Mom would interrupt whatever I was doing to get me to light whatever needed to be lit. Mom was always near while I did the lighting.

The thing that probably scared me the most was lighting the broiler in the old gas stove. I could get the match lit, but by the time I got the broiler turned on, the match would go out. By the time I finally got them synchronized, there would be enough gas buildup to give off a small explosion from the broiler, sometimes even burning the hair off of my arms.

After two weeks of match lighting, I was begging my mother to let me stop. I am still hesitant to light camp stoves or lanterns, and I'm sure this has something to do with my match-lighting training.

Today, I make a similar recommendation to parents of "budding pyromaniacs." We have to make adjustments to my mom's consequence because we don't light as many matches today as we used to. I suggest the following: make a plan with the child for when and where he can light matches.

Calmly ask Dennis, "Do you want to light one or two boxes of matches after school each day? Do you want to light them as soon as you get home or as soon as you've cleaned out your lunch bucket?" When the plan is made, put a rubber raincoat on the child, send him to the patio (or some other fireproofed surface) with a three-pound coffee can full of water. Tell him, "Now you can light the matches and throw them into the water to be safe. Call me if you would like me to watch."

When we do this, all of the power is taken out of the behavior. We are not screaming and yelling that they can't light matches when we know as well as they do that they can. The scare tactic of taking the child to the firehouse to see pictures of burned homes and/or people often has the opposite effect. It sometimes makes the "crime" even more exciting.

Thumb Sucking

Another habitual kind of behavior that gets to parents very quickly is thumb sucking. Years ago, I counseled with a couple who were getting very angry because their eight-year-old daughter, Hilary, was still sucking her thumb. I recommended that they give the girl a choice of sucking her thumb for 15 to 20 minutes per day in the family room as soon as she got home from school, or as soon as she changed her school clothes. Her choice was to do it for 20 minutes as soon as she got home from school. After that 20 minutes, any other thumb sucking would take place in her room. They would merely point to her room to indicate that she needed to go there for future thumb sucking. She was all excited about her new freedom, and the parents were confused with Dr. Platt's "nutty" recommendation.

"We are trying to get her to stop sucking her thumb, not give her permission to do it," they said. However, they did follow through with my recommendation.

The following day when she came home from school, she jumped up on the couch, and began sucking her thumb vigorously. Mother set the timer on the stove for 20 minutes, and then she went down the hallway to her bedroom because she was laughing hysterically. When Dad came home from work, he also observed his daughter sloshing away on her thumb and he, likewise, went to the bedroom where he began to laugh with his wife. Now, both Mom and Dad were laughing hysterically over a behavior that yesterday was evoking such anger in both of them. By the third day of the week, the girl was negotiating for 15 minutes of thumb sucking because she had other things she needed to do.

However, Mom replied in a very friendly voice, "Oh no, Dear; we can't do that! We agreed at Dr. John Platt's office that it would be 20 minutes a day. At the end of the week we can renegotiate." However, there was no need for any more negotiating because the girl no longer wanted to suck her thumb, at least not in Mom's and Dad's presence.

Whining Behavior

A woman who was a child care provider for eight four-year-olds took a class from me years ago. She was a large woman who was very firm but fair with the children, and did a marvelous job with them. Her biggest "bug button" was "mealy-mouthed" little people who cried and/or whined. So, of course, when these little persons wanted to get to her, all they had to do was whine. It drove her up the wall.

After we discussed how competent they were at getting to her, she set up the following plan. She gathered the children together and told them they really could whine better than any child care group before them. She said from now on she would not remind or scold them for whining. She would merely point to the "whining room" where any or all of them could go for their whining time.

Then she sat down with the children and they cut out pictures from magazines of children crying or whining, and taped them to the door of the "whining room."

The first day, all eight children were in the whining room doing what you do in a whining room. She could hear them saying, "Is she coming yet?" Then she realized who the whining behavior was for; after a few days, the whining stopped almost completely.

The "Who is Right" and "Who is Wrong" Power Struggle

"Who is right" and "who is wrong" have become hot issues in today's relationships.

Dr. Dreikurs suggested right and wrong issues have become a problem as a result of the movement toward equality. In the past, 50 to 60 years ago, right and wrong were never issues because the man was always right. The woman accepted (although she didn't necessarily like it) the fact that "Father knows best."

Today, this is not the case. Women want to be "more right" and therefore, the struggle for this position of superiority between men and women goes on. Children do not live in a vacuum. They see what's going on so they also decide to get into the struggle over who is right and who is wrong.

Often, what parents and children argue about is really not the issue, either. The issue is "who is right" and "who is wrong" or "who wins" and "who loses." Once again there is no winner in the power struggle.

In fact, when we argue with people we usually do two things. First, we convince them that they are more right than they were before the argument started. Any time you have to defend your position in the argument, you develop more ammunition for your cause.

The second possible outcome is to indicate to the other person that, "I'm really not too sure of my position in this argument." For example, Nick one day said to his dad, "I want to get a pool table."

Dad calmly replied, "Well, you can't afford to get a pool table, Nick. They're too expensive."

"But Dad," said Nick, "I saw one in the paper for $100.00."

Dad, feeling a bit tested, asked, "What do you mean? You can't even get a used table for $100.00."

"Dad, really I saw it in yesterday's paper," said Nick.

"Now listen to me, Nick. You are lying to me again," said Dad. And we all know where it goes from there.

An alternative parental stance might go like this:

"Dad, I want to get a pool table, and I saw one for $100.00 in the newspaper," said Nick.

Dad put down his newspaper and asked Nick, "How much do you have in savings?"

Nick looked at Dad and calmly answered, "About $180.00."

"Why don't you call and find out the particulars on the table? It sounds pretty inexpensive to me," said Dad.

I have found phrases like, "You may be right," or, "I never thought about it that way," or, "You have a point," or, "Maybe that's the way it is" to be neutral statements that say, "I'm not going to argue with you."

I was talking before a teachers' group a few years ago. We were discussing the "right and wrong issue" and how many relationships are literally torn apart by this battle. One of the teachers raised his hand and said, "If none of you will laugh at me, I'll tell you what my wife and I argued about last Friday evening and, as a result, didn't talk to each other for the rest of the weekend." Everyone agreed that nobody would laugh.

"We were arguing over what we would do with the California lottery money when we win it," he said with a silly grin. Of course, most people began to laugh and then someone said, "That sounds a lot like our house." It really does because we all get caught up in this issue in varying degrees of difficulty. We want so badly to be right and yet, what difference does it make anyway? Will it enhance our relationship if I am right, or will it help us be more miserable?

Fighting

One could write hundreds of pages on the importance of sibling fighting in the home. Many things are happening when we interfere in our children's fighting to determine who started it, how come, what for, and then punish the one the parent feels is to blame. (This is usually the older child in the family.)

Fighting has become more and more an issue in families as they get smaller and smaller. Fifty years ago when many families had eight to ten children, the children worked out their own differences. If Number Seven child went to Mom, who was making butter on the front porch, and reported that Number Five child had taken his hat, Mom said, "Well, you need to go get it back. I'm making butter." She didn't have time to get in the middle of all their fights; she was probably lucky if she knew all of their names. The children had to learn how to get along. Younger children learned they had better not "bug" their older siblings because *something* happened if they did.

I know personally about "bugging" older siblings because I was the second of two boys for eight years until my sister came along. I enjoyed aggravating my big brother. I saw him as almost invulnerable. He was a good student and athlete. I was neither a good student nor athlete, but I could break through this invulnerability by getting him to beat me up.

In those days, we always sat at the same place at the dinner table. I would sit directly across the table from my big brother. My dad sat next to my brother and my mom sat next to me to protect me from the "big ogre." All I had to do was put my foot on a brace that went down the middle of the table. I would wiggle the whole table. The milk would shimmy or the table would vibrate and my brother, with bulging veins in the side of his neck, would look across the table and tell me emphatically, "Get your foot down!"

I'd respond with this incredibly obnoxious smile that I used to infuriate him. After some thought, I would put my foot down but as I did it I would use my "smile" to aggravate him even more. This would continue four or five more times and then finally he would kick me under the table. That did it!

I would turn to my mother and in a whining, baby-talk voice say, "Momma, Charlie is kicking me under the table!"

Usually Mom would say, "Charles DeForest, go to your room."

My brother would get down from the table and go through the dining room door to his room, but he'd look back at me one more time. "I'm going to get you, you little sucker," he would mutter under his breath and I'd give him that same obnoxious smile one more time.

My brother jokingly says that today, as an adult, he still wakes up in the middle of the night and can see me smiling at him across the dinner table.

Therefore, I seldom have much sympathy for the younger one in a fight. They know exactly what to do to drive the older child up the wall. However, the results of taking the younger child's side against the older child are not so funny. Many older children in the family still harbor resentment toward the younger child years later.

A few years ago, I was teaching a week-long class on techniques for creating an encouraging atmosphere in the classroom to 34 teachers. A married couple, who were both teachers, told me of the concern they had for their gifted, older son, Paul, who was 11 years old and in the sixth grade. He had had poor performance in school the last four years. They were also concerned about the incessant fighting between him, and his younger sister, Suzie, who was 10 years old.

I asked them if I could interview the family in front of the class of teachers as the final experience of our week together. The parents were a little apprehensive because they knew all of the teachers in the class and it might be a little embarrassing. However, they agreed.

I talked first with the parents about the fighting and what we discovered was quite typical for most families. The older child gets in trouble and the younger one, who often instigates the disagreement, either gets off "Scot free" or is protected by the parents. However, we found that while Paul was incarcerated in his room for fighting, Suzie would walk back and forth outside his room saying, "Na, na, na, na; you're in your room," etc. Of course, Paul was infuriated by this and as soon as he was "released," he was back after his sister.

Talking with the children was helpful because during the discussion they clarified what was really going on. Suzie explained to me and the class of teachers that fighting was a "double-edged sword" for her because as she stated, "I love my brother but I love to see him in trouble."

The more we discussed their disagreements, the more it became evident how the fighting also influenced Paul's poor academic achievement. I asked him, "Is it possible, Paul, that you feel so hurt by the fact that Mom and Dad always take sides with Suzie when you two fight that you have decided to get back at Mom and Dad, who are both school teachers, by doing poorly in school?"

His face kind of "lit up" and he said emphatically, "Yes! I'm tired of always being the bad guy; it's not fair!"

We continued to discuss their fighting and I suggested that 20 or 30 years "down the road" they may still not like each other because of what was happening now. "There are many adults who really don't get along because of the very thing that's happening with you two right now," I said.

At this time, I happened to look out at the audience of teachers and I saw several pairs of pretty wet eyes.

Soon, the class was over, and afterwards four sets of wet eyes left immediately but three other sets came up to talk with me. One of the tearful people was a 60 year-old teacher who said, "After seeing this demonstration I am going home to write my brother a letter and tell him I am done fighting with him. We have been fighting each other for 58 years and it all began in almost the same way it has for Paul and Suzie."

I relate this story for two reasons. First, it demonstrates how fighting is not just a "here and now" dispute. It can, and often does, have an effect on many other areas such as Paul's poor performance, and it can seriously affect how siblings get along later in their lives.

Most of the time, we parent in reverse. When the children act like human beings we move away from them. When they act like little monsters we move toward them. I often ask children who fight a lot, "What does Mom or Dad do when you play quietly together?"

"They go get dinner started or get some work done," they'll say.

"Well, what do they do when you fight?" I'll ask.

In unison, they'll answer very emphatically, "Oh, they come to us!"

"It sounds like the name of the game is to hit your brother and call your mother," I'll say, and they both nod their heads and grin. It is often easier to see this in other families than in our own.

Parents are convinced that if they stay out of their children's fights, the older child will kill the younger one. I often ask parents if they are around the children all of the time. "Of course," they tell me, "that would be impossible." I suggest that if the children wanted to kill each other, they would do it when Mom and Dad weren't around. I try to lessen parents' worrying about bodily harm being done by telling them , "I have given this recommendation (to stay out of kid's fights) for 25 years now and we've only had two deaths." They laugh and relax and begin to see fighting as not such an astronomical problem.

Setting an Older Sibling Up

A common scenario in many homes may go something like this:

At 2:50 p.m., the Younger One checks the kitchen clock because he knows his older brother will be home at 3:00 p.m. (This is how younger children in the family learn to tell time.) He says to himself, "I'd better get busy; I only have ten minutes to get my work done." The Younger One slithers down the hall to the Older One's bedroom.

He enters the room and merely moves a few of older brother's possessions to a different place. Finally, the Younger One hears his brother come home, so he goes across the hallway into Mom's and Dad's bedroom and waits patiently for the ensuing onslaught.

The Older One goes into his room, checks it out, and sees that some of his possessions have been moved. Then he begins to look for the perpetrator of this crime. He knows where his little brother is, because he is always in the same place. The Older One goes across the hallway into Mom's and Dad's bedroom and finds the culprit.

The Older One says, "I have had it with you; I told you to stay out of my room and now I am going to kill you again."

Big brother raises his fist to destroy the younger brother and the Younger One lets off a horrendous scream (youngest children have large lungs) and shrieks, "Mama, Mama, he's going to kill me again."

At this time the dispenser of love, justice, and brotherhood, as well as prosecuting attorney, juror, parole/probation officer, cook, and chauffeur comes running down the hallway yelling at the top of her voice, "This is a house of love!"

When she gets into the bedroom, she zeros in on the Older One! The Older One is saying, "Just wait, Mom. I've tried to get him to stay out of my room. I've paid him money; I've given him candy. I've put a lock on my door, and he comes in through my window."

Mom gets into a "I-told-you-so" parenting posture (hands on hips, and shoulders stooped a little) and she says, "When you were his age, you did exactly the same kind of things. You should be more responsible and set an example. After all, you are Older. He doesn't know that jumping up and down on your Bruce Springsteen record makes you mad. He's only 14."

Now the Younger One is standing behind Mom flipping his older brother off or using the famous obnoxious smile. As soon as Mom is out of the way and not there to protect the younger one, they go back to fighting.

When we interfere in children's fights and protect the Younger One from the Older One, we are not improving their relationship; we are hurting it. The Older One can become resentful and hurtful because he is always in trouble and the Younger One is learning the discouraging lesson that "someone will always protect me even when I start something." This is often the thinking of a person who develops a victim's outlook on life.

Some Ways to Handle Fighting

My suggestion to parents is that there are many options to dealing with children's fighting in the family. The most effective way is to discuss disagreements at a family meeting, or to talk specifically with each combatant about alternatives. The younger one might want to quit bugging the older one or vice versa. If the fighting is really bad, the younger one might want to put a lock on his door. He might want to ask the older one to do something for fun.

A discussion with the older child might include how much the younger one wants the big brother's or sister's attention. If the older one would do something with the younger one in a positive, constructive way, maybe the younger one wouldn't continue "bugging" his older sibling so much.

However, the following four recommendations can be used with or without the family meeting: (1) Ignore the fighting (which I have found to be very difficult to do); (2) give the children the choice of continuing their disagreement, verbal or physical, in the garage or the backyard; (3) separate and send them to their rooms, and (4) the most effective option is to completely withdraw to another place in the home when the fighting starts, or as Dreikurs recommended, "Go to the bathroom."

There are two realities of which children are very aware. Parents cannot stop children from fighting for any length of time and parents don't like to hear what happens when their children fight. When parents have the children leave or they leave, they recognize these two realities.

It is respectful and encouraging for children to learn they can work out their problems with each other. They don't have to have a parent in the middle trying to always make things "better."

Fighting in the Car

I am often asked, "What do we do when children are fighting in the car and we can't stay out of it because it is dangerous to drive when we are being distracted by the commotion?"

There are many things that the parent can do. Pulling off the road, stopping on the side of the road and stating, "I'll drive when it's quiet and safe" would be one parent stance.

While parked beside the road, the parent can ask the combatants to get out of the car to "work it out." Or the parent can get out until it is peaceful.

When I coached wrestling, we made long trips with 50 wrestlers in a school bus. The bus driver and I made an agreement that whenever "monkey business" or rough housing started in the bus, we would stop. It was amazing how well-mannered the bus riders became when the driver just put her foot on the brake!

Another alternative is to discuss this problem at a family meeting. What ideas do the children have for resolving fighting in the car? Some options we learned from our own children were:

(1) Rotate who sits where in the car. Our children asked us if it was some part of our cultural heritage that mothers and fathers had to sit in the front seat. Maybe a child could sit "front seat by the window." This rotation system was especially helpful for long trips.

(2) Have a spiral notebook in the glove compartment that has the order of rotation listed. People with large families find this helpful because it is difficult to remember who sat where. Keeping this notebook can prevent disharmony.

I found when living in the Los Angeles area that when parents practiced the above techniques, their children would not fight on surface streets but only on the freeways. The children, of course, realized that it was much more difficult for parents to stop on the freeways. However, there are always off ramps!

Questions

1) What did Dreikurs mean when he said a misbehaving child is a discouraged child? pp. 44 - 45

2) Why does the author believe there is optimism in recognizing the four goals of mistaken behavior? p. 44

3) Why is our first reaction to the child's mistaken behavior usually ineffective? p. 45

4) How can a parent or teacher diagnose which of the four goals the child is using? p. 45

5) Who wins the power struggle? Why? p. 47

6) What must the adult do when he/she is involved in the power or revenge cycle with the child? p. 47

7) Why is asking oneself, "What can I do in this situation?" an encouraging decision? p. 49

8) What is suggested as a method of dealing with children that display the goal of inadequacy? p. 49

9) Think of some statements your children make that push the "bug button"? Now, referring to p. 48, list some responses you could make to those statements. p. 53

10) In helping a child set up a homework time, what three choices could the parent use? p. 54

11) What are the three things a parent needs to do in order to help students to be responsible for their homework? p. 54

12) What is the author's rule of thumb for a parent to deal with a child who is lying? p. 56

13) Why is it so difficult for parents to handle lying? p. 56

14) What happens to children's need for power when we give them permission to do "forbidden" things? p. 59

15) Why does the debate over "who is right and who is wrong?" become such an issues? p. 62

16) Why does the author have such little sympathy for the young child in the dispute? p. 65

17) Why is it so important for our children's future relationships that we stay out of their fights? p. 67

18) What does the author mean when he says, "we parent in reverse"? p. 67

19) What lesson is the younger child learning when we protect him/ her from the older one? p. 69

20) What four options do we have in dealing with children? p. 69

21) What does the author suggest for dealing with children's fighting in the car? p. 70

PUNISHMENT HAS LOST ITS EFFECTIVENESS 5

"If punishing, hitting, or yelling at kids worked, I'd be out of a job."
—John Platt, Ed.D.
Marriage and Family Counselor

In an autocratic society punishment and reward were somewhat effective methods for managing children. However, since we are becoming more egalitarian and thus, democratic, in our society, we are finding that the old methods based on "inferior-superior" relationships do not work.

The problem with using a punishment system with today's children is that they believe if adults have the *right* to punish them, they have the *right* to punish the adult. This can end in a power or revenge cycle where there are no winners. I see families being ripped apart by these struggles where children and parents pull out all stops to win or get even.

So many parents with whom I counsel believe that if they just punish harder, the child will *finally* learn. But when I ask the parent if spanking the child is an effective means of discipline, they almost always say "no." Part of this is the traditional style with which most parents were raised. The only alternative they know for not punishing the child is to let the child do anything he wants without something negative happening.

After a speech I gave to a parent's group at an elementary school, a tall, athletic-looking woman approached me. As part of my presentation, I had discussed the futility of using punishment to influence our children. The woman explained that she had a fourteen month-old son who kept sticking his fingers into light sockets. She, of course, didn't want him to electrocute himself, so she would go to him, say "no" and slap his hand. After a week of this method, she moved towards him to discipline him again for the same behavior. However, before she could slap his hand, he struck her. She was shocked and could not believe he would do this. Can you imagine what this child will be like during his teenage years if Mom continues to punish him this way?

The alternative method for punishment is the use of logical consequences. This idea is not new; Aristotle talked about logical punishment. It is very much like Dreikurs' logical consequences concept.

The following page shows a list of the differences between logical consequences and punishment.

Logical consequences allow mutual respect to be maintained. It is important to note that when the misbehavior is a recurring one, such as an eating problem, the consequence can be discussed in a calm moment with the child. It is important to use limited choices (page 23) when setting up the consequence with the child. Asking the child, "Do you want to eat quietly or get down from the table?" gives the opportunity for the child to choose the behavior and/or the consequence when the situation arises again. Talking with the child regarding a specific consequence is an example of being *proactive* versus being *reactive*. We are usually reacting to the misbehavior rather than making a plan for future situations.

Thus, we don't have to use the "I told you so" morally superior stand. The attitude of the parent is one of mild regret over what has happened, but the next time the child might make a more appropriate choice! *When helping parents figure out a logical consequence, as a rule of thumb, I suggest that the parents put themselves in the child's situation.* What would be logical for the adult would also be logical

COMPARISON OF LOGICAL
CONSEQUENCES AND PUNISHMENT

LOGICAL CONSEQUENCE(S) VS PUNISHMENT

	LOGICAL CONSEQUENCE(S)		PUNISHMENT
1.	Reality of the situation trains the child: situation-centered.	1.	Power of authority dominates: self-centered.
2.	Related logically to the behavior.	2.	Usually arbitrary, little logic.
3.	No element of moral judgment: good or bad, right or wrong.	3.	Some moral judgment: usually "bad" or "wrong."
4.	Deals with what will happen now.	4.	Deals with the past.
5.	Teaches child to be responsible for own behavior.	5.	Implies the adult is responsible for child's behavior.
6.	Develops inner-discipline.	6.	Outer-discipline maintained.
7.	Adult remains friendly; positive atmosphere maintained.	7.	Adult displays anger; antagonistic atmosphere remains.
8.	Influences or leads child toward more desirable behavior; training for the future.	8.	Forces or "makes" child obey; is usually only temporary.

for the child. For example, if Mom spills milk, she cleans it up. If Dad breaks a lamp, he buys a new one. If cousin Chris wets his bed, he changes the sheets. If Dad missed his bus to work, he would have to pay taxi fare. If Uncle Steve forgets his lunch, he goes hungry or borrows from someone else. This one rule of thumb is helpful in figuring out what a logical consequence might be for the child.

If the parent's motivation for carrying out the consequence is to make the child suffer, probably no suffering will take place. The reason children are excused from the table is because fighting at a dinner meal is inappropriate behavior. Many times the child might say, "I'm full anyway, so I don't care if I have to get down." In other words, if the logical consequence is just another way to make a child behave, it will more likely be met with defiance.

A logical consequence should not be used in a dangerous situation. "If you stay in the street, the Mac truck will hit you" is not a responsible parental stance.

The following are examples of logical consequences that I have either recommended, or learned from parents over the last 25 years.

Sally's Lunch

Almost every day, Sally would forget the lunch her mother made for her. Mother would take the lunch to school (as most "good" mothers do.) After learning about logical consequences, Mom in a very friendly but firm voice, explained to Sally, "I am not going to bring your lunch anymore. I really believe I am being disrespectful of you when I do something for you that I know you can do for yourself."

Sally continued to forget her lunch a few more times because her friends would share their lunches. However, when they got tired of sharing, Sally began to remember to take her own lunch.

Restuarant Consequence

A friend of mine, from a family of six children, told me how her father handled the children's misbehavior *one time*, and only one time, at a restaurant. Dad was a laborer; therefore, money was at a premium. Going out to dinner was a twice-a-year occasion. I asked my friend if it wasn't like a zoo, going out to dinner with such a large family. She said "no" and then told me what happened on one occasion.

They arrived at the restaurant, ordered their meals and the waitress brought their food. One of the children poured ketchup in someone's milk, and that was the beginning of "some upheaval."

Dad simply signaled to the waitress to come back to the table, and he whispered something in her ear. A few minutes later, she came back with a plastic garbage sack.

Dad asked each child to pass his plate of food to him. Dad proceeded to dump the food into the garbage sack until no food was on the table. He got up from the table and said, "Let's go."

They all followed him out to their VW bus, got in, and went home. When they arrived home, Dad got out the turkey platter and poured all the food on the platter.

He said, "This is our dinner out."

Some might say he was certainly harsh with those children. I believe he was respectful. He didn't threaten, cajole, warn, or get angry; he just acted. He might have told them before they went to the restaurant that this was what he was going to do. I didn't have to ask my friend how they behaved at a restaurant after that; the answer was obvious. It is so important to act, not talk. This is exactly what that father did.

Bed-Wetting

One of our sons had a serious lung infection when he was about three years old. As a result, he spent almost a month in a children's hospital. Since his lung had collapsed, they did not want him to cry. Consequently, they indulged him to no end. When he came home, we thought "Attila the Hun" had been resurrected. Besides wanting his own way about everything, he went back to wetting his bed (he had been toilet trained for nearly a year). Ann and I would change his sheets and try not to show how frustrated we were. However, the bed wetting continued.

During this time, at one of our family meetings, one of the other two boys looked at our bed-wetting son and said, "Do you know how not to wet the bed?"

The three-year-old smiled and nodded.

Then the other son recommended that since he knew how *not* to wet the bed, he could change and wash his own sheets. We accepted that recommendation.

From then on, he would take the sheets off every morning and put them in the washing machine. After that, he would drag them out into the gravel backyard (we lived in Tucson at the time) and crawl up on his trike with the sheets.

He would often forget the clothes pins, so down again he would go. Once he was back up on the trike, he would have the clothes pins, but no sheet. By the time he got the sheets hung up, they were almost dry. Later, he would take them down, bring them back into the house, and we would help him put them back on the bed.

For five or six days, he loved it. Starting the washing machine was great fun. We thought he liked this so much, he'd never stop wetting the bed. But before long the newness wore off, and he got tired of spending most of his morning changing sheets. Within a week, he stopped wetting the bed and never did it again.

The Morning Routine

As I have mentioned previously, Ann and I had the opportunity to study with Dr. Rudolf Dreikurs in Oregon from 1960 to 1968 during summer schools. He would always say, "The most important meal in the day is breakfast."

I debated that dinner was the most important meal because the family could share with each other what happened during the day. The longer I am a family counselor, however, the more I realize how correct Dreikurs was. If we can have a pleasant five or ten-minute breakfast together and start the day off in a positive way, it can affect how the rest of the day goes. Parents are so busy, especially when both are working outside the home, that just getting out the door without some kind of disagreement is unusual. Therefore, this positive breakfast time is even more important.

The morning routine in most families is a disaster. Between 75% to 80% of the families in the United States wake up with a fight. We can't get up and go off to school without some kind of hassle. I have recommended the following action which has been helpful to many families:

The child could be given an inexpensive electric alarm clock and the choice of getting up at 7:00 a.m. or 7:05 a.m. Breakfast will be served (attended by as many members of the family as possible) between 7:30 a.m. and 7:50 a.m. The child will need to be dressed before he comes to breakfast.

However, if the child decides "I'm not getting up. I'm not eating breakfast!" then the parent merely goes to the child's room ten minutes before departure time and puts the child's clothes in a paper bag. "You may dress on the way to preschool, or get dressed now during the remaining ten minutes you have. We'll be leaving in ten minutes." If the child chooses to do neither, the consequence will be getting dressed at preschool.

As I have mentioned before, it is important to explain this whole process to the child before you carry it out. In this way, the child can make the decision. Again, the purpose for doing it this way is so the parent doesn't have to scream, yell, or humiliate the child. It is more respectful of the child to believe he is able to get out of bed, dress himself, get to breakfast, and remember what he needs to take to preschool, or child care or school.

School Skipping

The following is an example of a logical consequence my mother used with me when I was 15 years-old.

Frequently, I would stay home on Friday (test day) so I could get the test questions from my friends; then I could barely pass the make-up test on Monday. Since my mom worked outside the home, sometimes I would leave to go to school only to come back after she had gone. This was many years ago when people did not walk around the streets when they skipped school. You hid where you would be "safe."

One time, I stayed home and Mom returned from work because she had forgotten something. She found me at home. I was shocked to find that she had returned, and when she asked me why I was not in school, I told her that I was sick.

My mother said, "Well, you don't look very good, John Murray. I think you better get upstairs and get into bed right now." I knew that my bubble was popped when my mother came into my room with a thermometer. After she had taken my temperature she looked concerned. Maybe I really was sick!

I had to get into bed immediately and stay there all day. We had no television, so that was not an issue.

Mom called her boss to tell him she had to stay home with her "sick" child. During the day she brought me a lot of water to drink, but no food. I had vomited according to my story and she didn't want to further upset my stomach. That evening, about 12 hours later, I received one-half of a slice of toast with nothing on it. By noon the following day, Mom brought me a couple of pieces of toast and some hot, black, sugarless tea. By Saturday evening, I was eating chicken broth, or rather, inhaling it. After this happened, I never got "sick" on Friday again.

When I counsel parents of "school-phobic" children, I often tell the parents that story. School phobia, from my point of view, is often a demonstration of power on the child's part, or of doing "what I want, when I want, and where I want." I find that if the parent or child-care person follows through on the above recommendation, it could have a profound effect on the child's decision to return to school.

Cleaning Up One's Own Mess

There was a single-parent mother I remember who took a parenting class from me a few years ago. She lived in a low-income housing complex, and was fearful she might be asked to leave the apartment because of her destructive five year-old's behavior. He wrote on both the outside and inside walls, broke things and generally dismantled the complex.

One day, he found some colored chalk and began drawing all over the sidewalk outside their apartment. Mother would usually get very angry and swat him, yell at him, or shake him. Now, with her new technique utilizing logical consequences, she very calmly asked him if he wanted to clean up the "chalk art" right now or as soon as Sesame Street was over. "Right now," he said. She then got him a bucket with soapy water and a brush and accompanied him to the scene of the crime. He began to scrub the chalk. The first 15 minutes he enjoyed himself. During the last 45 minutes of the clean-up process, the joy of the activity left. He finally got it done, came in the house and said, "I don't think I'll write on the sidewalk anymore, Mom." Mother was much encouraged because it "worked," and the best part was she didn't have to feel guilty for hitting him.

Logical consequences can help reduce the hurtful feelings that occur when punishment is used. Also, using logical consequences helps the child see the consequence as being fair and thus, the need to retaliate can be reduced dramatically. The child can develop into the cooperative human being he wants to become.

Grounding

Grounding has been used for years to punish children for all sorts of "sins." It is the belief of many adults that taking time away from the child to spend with friends, or not letting them talk on the phone, or taking away the child's chance to participate in a school function will encourage the child to behave in a more productive way.

Sometimes children will respond to the grounding but oftentimes they see it as just more punishment. They respond to the grounding by fighting back or trying to get even.

Not only do children get grounded for everything, they often get grounded forever. I asked an eight-year-old misbehaving child, "How long have you been grounded?"

"I'm grounded until I am 21 years old," he answered.

It almost sounded like life in prison with no chance for parole.

Many times when the child is grounded, he has no idea what he has to do to be "ungrounded." I asked that same eight year-old what he needed to do to be taken off the grounding and he replied, "My dad just said I have to shape up."

When I asked him what that meant, he said, "I don't know." However, his parent felt he should know!! After all, he needs to get better grades in school, finish doing his chores on time and quit beating up on his brother!

I believe grounding can be a logical consequence in some situations. Grounding is related to misbehaviors such as: coming home late after school, violating a curfew agreement, or being drunk or stoned. It is logical to not be able to go out the rest of the weekend or not drive the car for two months. Grounding is not logical when it is used to punish children for fighting, not cleaning their rooms, or talking back and lying.

As an example, if the child does violate a curfew agreement, I would recommend that Mom tell Joey, "You were late last weekend and you are now asking to go to the dance after the football game. Since the dance is over at 11:00 p.m., do you want to come home at 11:30 p.m. or at 12:00 midnight?"

Joey could reply, "That's silly, Mom. Midnight, of course!"

"If you violate our agreement to come home at midnight, would you like to stay home one weekend or two?" asked Mom.

Joey can easily reply, "That's silly, too. One weekend."

If he comes home even a few minutes late without calling to explain his tardiness, Mom doesn't have to get upset or scream and yell. All Mom has to say is, "I'm sorry you're late; we'll talk about it in the morning."

In the morning, Mom would merely confirm Joey's choice to stay home one weekend and there is no need for arguing, moralizing, or lecturing.

Grounding should be used sparingly and only when there is some logic to its use.

Safety Deposit Box

Years ago, when our children were quite young, we decided at a family meeting that we were going to use a "deposit box" to help keep the living area in the house picked up. We tried many "systems" with this approach. For instance, you could not get back your things for a three-day or one-week period, or you were fined a certain amount per article. However, we found we were getting into a record keeping system that took more time than it was worth.

The two reasons we implemented the "safety deposit box" were (1) to reduce the amount of nagging from the parents, and (2) to get the living areas in order. After many discussions at family meetings, we decided on the following: there would be a deposit box (a big one at first) out in the garage. Anyone at anytime could put anything they found lying around the common areas of the house in the "safety deposit box." Each member of the family could go get their "stuff" whenever he found it missing.

Father learned a great deal from the use of the family "safety deposit box." Early in our marriage, I would leave my clothes around and it would be very upsetting to Ann; however, a few weeks after we implemented the "new system," my favorite wearing apparel (my coach's coat with "Coach Platt" embroidered on it) was missing. I didn't say anything because I often lose things and therefore didn't even want to bring it up. After a few days, I thought about the "safety deposit box." I went to the garage and there in the box was my coach's jacket! This happened almost 25 years ago. To this day, as soon as I get home from work, I go right to our bedroom and hang up the clothes I can wear again, put others in the laundry, and change into leisure clothes. The "safety deposit box" has helped strengthen our marriage—not just teach the children to pick up their stuff!

Questions

1) Why is the use of punishment in training children becoming less and less effective? p. 73

2) What do many parents believe is the only alternative to punishing a child? p. 73

3) Is the idea of logical consequences a new idea? p. 74

4) How can a parent be proactive in setting up a logical consequence? p. 74

5) What rule of thumb can we keep in mind when setting up a logical consequence? p. 74

6) When should we never use logical consequences? p. 76

7) What are suggestions for dealing with a child who has recurring bedwetting problems? pp. 77 -78

8) Why did Dreikurs suggest that breakfast is the most important meal of the day? p. 78

9) What happens too often when we use grounding as a logical consequence? p. 81

10) How can grounding be a logical consequence in some instances? p. 82

11) What are two reasons for implementing the "deposit box"? p. 83

ENCOURAGEMENT 6

"A child (human being) needs
encouragement like a plant needs water."
—Rudolf Dreikurs

The most important puzzle piece of effective, positive parenting is learning the art of encouragement. Yet, this is the most difficult part.

As we become more egalitarian and, thus, move toward a democratic society, the reward system loses its effectiveness in stimulating positive behaviors in our children. Just like punishment, children do not see a bribe or a reward as a privilege handed down from the 'superior' adult to the 'inferior' child. Instead, children see the reward as their right.

A friend of mine learned the futility of rewards when he gave his seven year-old daughter, Julie, 10¢ to clean her room every day. She loved this and was happy to build up her bank account. However, this lasted only two weeks. Then one morning Julie came out of her bedroom and told her father that she now wanted 15¢ for cleaning her room because she had learned to do a much better job. This was not a negotiation based on an "inferior-superior" relationship.

Dad became even more frustrated with this outdated system when Julie came out one sunny morning and hadn't even bothered to clean her room.

"Julie, you don't get your 15¢ this morning because you didn't clean your room," Dad said in an exasperated voice.

"Oh, I have enough money, Dad," said Julie with an upturned nose. "I don't care about the 15¢ anymore."

Needless to say, Dad felt angry and frustrated because the reward system was bankrupt. Another drawback to the reward system is that children quickly learn that in order to get a reward you sometimes have to misbehave.

I worked with a gifted high school senior who was ready to flunk out of high school. He had been almost a straight "A" student until his first year in junior high when he faltered and got a few B's and B-'s. From then on, until his senior year, his grades charted something like this:

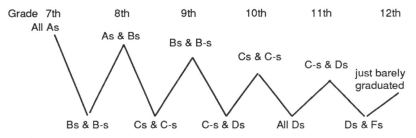

I asked him why his grades were so erratic, up and down so much. He matter-of-factly told me, "The first dip to B's and B-'s was in the 7th grade and then when I got it back up to A's and B's, I got my first dirt bike."

It turned out the next setback in the 8th grade was rewarded by yet another, but more powerful, motorbike. As he progressed into high school, he was rewarded with cars and other desirable materialistic items to get his grades "up." He had figured out the reward system but definitely not to his long-range advantage.

In my practice, and while speaking to schools and other public institutions, I see this happening more and more with our children. Today's child feels that, "I will do nothing unless I get something for it."

The Definition of Encouragement

We often hear definitions of self-esteem and self-concept that are quite complex. If Adler's and Dreikurs' concept that human beings are social beings and that they want to belong is corrrect, then I believe the definition of encouragement is helping children feel a sense of belonging and competency. We need to create ways for our children to have a chance to contribute.

The idea that misbehaving children are discouraged children is often difficult to accept. They are discouraged because they cannot find their place or have a sense of belonging in a useful, contributing way. As we have discussed in the chapter on the four mistaken goals, the only way these discouraged children believe they can be significant is through useless and destructive kinds of behavior.

On New Year's Day, in 1989, there was a short piece on television about a 17 year-old Mexican-American boy who arrived in the United States with his mother in 1987. Shortly after his arrival, he joined a gang in East Los Angeles and immediately started getting into serious trouble. A teacher at the high school he attended asked him to be a Spanish translator in a school for Spanish-speaking, retarded children a couple of days a week. He did this and soon began getting involved in other volunteer work. He eventually won an award for being the most helpful volunteer in the Los Angeles schools, and was honored at a city-wide banquet. He left the gang to become a really productive and encouraged member of society.

When he was interviewed, his answers sounded as if he had studied with Adler or Dreikurs.

"Why did you join the gangs, Antonio?" the interviewer asked him. He paused a moment, and said, "Because I had no sense of belonging. Hanging out with the gang helped me feel accepted."

Antonio was asked why translating for Spanish-speaking children helped him. "Because I really felt I was making a contribution and it felt good," he said.

The concept of encouragement is not what is difficult. Making statements and doing specific behaviors that are encouraging to others are more difficult because we are usually not trained to do this.

We need to stop discouraging

When I do workshops with parents, I like to have them list things they say and do that are either discouraging or encouraging. Sometimes we think we have been encouraging but we are not.

The following discouraging behaviors are common ones listed by parents:

1.   Calling children names or labeling them as lazy, stupid, hyperactive, tired, etc.

2.   Doing for children what they can do for themselves, such as dressing, feeding, or doing a project for school.

3.   Being a constant critic of their efforts.

4.   Giving children conditional approval by saying things like, "The bed is neatly made but look at the rest of this messy room," or, "Thanks for cleaning the kitchen, but can't you ever get the stove cleaned right?" and "If you'd just try harder you could do better. You're really not working up to your potential." This statement is often made by parents to encourage.

5.   Comparing children to their siblings or to other children their age. Statements like,"If you'd just try harder you could do math just like your sister" are not encouraging. Additionally, the message the children receive is, "You have little worth as you are. When you are a better person, I will accept you." I suggest using that statement with another adult and seeing if it sounds like encouragement. "You know, Mrs. Smith, if you'd just try harder you could be a decent parent."

6.   Having either too high or too low expectations for children.

7.   Being overprotective or indulgent and not letting children experience the consequences of their choices. It is disrespectful and a discouraging way to treat our children. We believe by indulging our children and getting them whatever they want they will definitely be happy, but all they really learn is, "if I can't have what I want whenever I want it, I'll never be happy."

8.   Feeling sorry for or pitying a child are really discouraging

kinds of behaviors and feelings. The message of pity is, "You poor thing, life is so tough. I know you'll never be able to handle it."

9. Using superlative words such as "great," "wonderful," "super," and "excellent" are usually not encouraging.

10. Showing children by what we say and do that we don't need them. Here we are back to our original definition of encouragement: *belonging* and *feeling competent.*

How then do we give our children the chance to develop this sense of belonging and feeling competent? Before discussing some specific techniques for encouragement, I would like to share a very helpful chart comparing praise/reward and encouragement as developed by Bonnie Sanders and Julie Dixon. The "rules of thumb" they suggest are very helpful in understanding encouragement. (See Chart p. 90)

Specific Techniques for Encouraging Children:

1. It is important to use phrases that build the child's sense of belonging and feeling competent. The following examples demonstrate this concept:

"Thank you for your help in setting the table."

"I enjoyed our walk together last night."

"Helping your brother learn to read is such a nice contribution to all of us as a family."

"Your drawing has so many pretty colors. I will put it on the refrigerator so we can all enjoy it."

"It certainly was enjoyable to go out together to dinner last night."

"It is enjoyable for me to see how much fun you have playing baseball."

"I noticed how well you worked to get your room picked up."

"Help me make a plan for tonight's meal."

"It's pretty difficult to do, but I believe you can handle it."

2. Creating specific ways to need our children is encouraging. The following are some examples:

DIFFERENCES BETWEEN PRAISE AND ENCOURAGEMENT
by Bonnie G. Sanders & Judi Dixon

	PRAISE	ENCOURAGEMENT
Definition (from Webster's New Collegiate Dictionary, 1977):	(1) to express a favorable judgement of (2) to glorify, especially by attribution of perfection (3) an expression of approval	(1) to inspire with courage, spirit or hope: Hearten (2) to spur on: Stimulate
helpful hint:	P — Praise, focus on Person	E — Encouragement, focus on Effort
focus of control:	outer, external	inner, self
recognizes:	only complete, perfect product only winners get praise (reward)	effort and improvement, used when child not doing well
relys/depends on:	(approval from) others evaluation	(approval from) self evaluation
effects on self-esteem	feels worthwhile only when others approve, say so	feels worthwhile as she/he is without others approval
attitude:	patronizing, expectant	respectful, appreciative giving a compliment without sense of controlling
question (it may be helpful):	"Would I say this or make this comment to a colleague or friend?" If not, it is probably praise	"Would I say this or make this comment to a colleague or friend," it is probably encouragement
used most often with:	children (We've often heard, "You're a good girl/boy for clearing the table"; but how often have you heard, "You're a good wo/man for clearing the table"???)	adults (We usually say "Thank you. I appreciate your help." or "That was a big help.")
examples:	"I'm proud of you for . . . . . . getting a good report card". . . . making an 'A' in math". (robs person of ownership of own achievement)	"You must be proud of . . . . . . yourself/your report card." . . . your improvement in math." (recognizes ownership and responsibility of achievement)

a. Setting up a Chore Chart with jobs that are significant and at the proper developmental level of the child. See Chapter 1 for setting up a Chore Chart and Appendix for a list of chores children of different ages can do.

b. Including children in the planning of upcoming events such as going shopping, going on vacation, or organizing a party. This can be done at the family meeting.

c. Allowing children to be helpers and teachers of younger children.

3. Helping children learn that it is O.K. to make a mistake. Our society is so perfectionistically-oriented that all of us have a hard time accepting mistakes. Children learn a lot by observing an adult's reaction to various situations. When parents put themselves or others down for making mistakes, children often follow this example. When we break an egg or spill something, we usually say something like, "Oh, great! There I go again. Another day like yesterday! Eggs are so expensive and here I am dropping them on the floor." We might say instead, "Oh, that will make a nice breakfast for the dog. Fido, come here and enjoy an egg."

Sometimes with the perfectionistic child we may overdo our efforts to be encouraging. We might say, for example, "Honey, I like the yellow sun. It really brightens up your drawing."

The perfectionistic child will sometimes answer, "But I don't like it, Mom, because the yellow crayon went out the lines on the sun."

Mom hangs in there and answers, "Yes, dear, but I still like it."

The determined, perfectionistic child will complain, "But Mom, it doesn't look right that way!"

Mom, in an angry voice, says, "Well, I like it and it's tough luck if you don't like it!"

The same scenario might also go like this:

"Honey, I like the yellow sun. It really brightens up your drawing," says Mom.

"But I don't like it, Mom, because the yellow crayon went out of the lines on the sun," pouts the perfectionistic child.

"I'm sorry you don't like it, but since I do, I think I'll go ahead and put it up on the refrigerator," says the encouraging mother.

4.   It is important to build on strengths and not on weaknesses. A parent could say, "You really hit that ball the second time up to bat! I'll bet that felt good," rather than "You did hit the ball, but you've really got to work on your fielding. You made three errors today."

When I was coaching high school wrestling in Oregon, I discovered that I didn't have to tell the wrestlers what they did wrong; they already knew. I had to help them see their strengths in their athletic performances. After they finished wrestling their match, I would hand them a clipboard with a chart on it. On one side of the chart was written, "What did I do well and what did I improve on from my last match?" On the other side of the chart was, "What areas do I need to work on for my next match?" When I first started this exercise, the wrestlers would have almost the exact list I had for "areas I need to work on" but listed almost nothing on the "what did I do well?" side.

It took a while for the wrestlers to begin recognizing their strengths, and as they learned to do this, their performances improved dramatically. The goal was to have everyone on the team do the best he could rather than be so over concerned about winning. When you have everyone on the team doing the best he can do, regardless of his athletic ability, guess what? You win! We won two state championships in Oregon before the wrestlers really began to believe that the improvement of their performance is the most important thing, not just winning. That's almost un-American!!!

5.   Rather than doing everything for children that they can do for themselves, encourage them in their efforts to dress themselves, repair their own bikes, pour the milk, or do the wash. Genuine happiness comes from developing self-sufficiency, not from being overprotected and indulged.

6.   Staying out of children's fights or allowing them to work out their differences is encouraging. Working to reduce fighting can be done at a family meeting. It demonstrates respect for the children and that we really do believe they can resolve their own differences. (See

Section on "Fighting.")

7. Having "Special Time" with our children is encouraging. (See sections on "Special Time" and "Communicating with Our Children.")

8. It is important to take time to train the child before setting expectations of his performance on certain tasks. When we want a child to clean his room, we need to demonstrate what that means. A clean room to a child is often very different from what a clean room is to a perfectionistic adult. We also need to help create a room where it is possible for the child to be successful in cleaning it up. Some ways to do this are by placing the clothing bar in the closet at a level the child can reach, by reducing the number of toys the child has so he can organize them on shelves that are at his level, and by providing areas to store toys. These are all ways to increase the child's potential for keeping a room in some semblance of order.

9. One of my favorite "techniques" for encouraging others and one's self is to write what I call a "letter of encouragement." As a high school teacher in Oregon in the 1960s, I found that sending home failing notices was totally ineffective, so I decided to write letters of encouragement. The following are ideas to consider when writing an encouraging note:

   a. The statement needs to be truthful and specific.
   b. Use phrases that recognize the child's contribution to the family or to us as parents such as: "I appreciate your efforts last night in getting the dishes done" or "It was nice going for a walk with you last night."

Writing and receiving a letter can be much more encouraging than verbal statements. You can read the letter over and over and even laminate it if you want. Often our children don't hear us even when we say something positive. Letters demonstrate to children that they are worth our taking the time and making the effort to write a note. I really believe it is as encouraging to the person who writes the note as it is to the person who receives it. Children soon realize that giving to others feels good.

Gail Golomb wrote the following letter of encouragement to her nine year-old daughter, Jennifer. "Dear Jennifer: I am a very lucky Mom to have a wonderful and loving daughter like you! I love the way you smile and I love to hear your giggles and laughter. You are very funny and make me laugh. You also ask lots of interesting questions to keep me on my toes. I love the way you care about your friends, and your brother, too. You have a special place in your heart for other people's feelings. I love how you care about animals and make sure they are safe. I love the way you care about school and that you do your very best. Most of all, I love you, Jennifer, for being you!"

The next night, Mom found on her pillow a letter from Jennifer. It read, "Sweet dreames, Mom."

Encouragement is Discipline

It is important to keep in mind that every time we encourage children we are *disciplining* them. Encouraged children do not strike out and hurt others, or need to be the boss, or want someone's attention at all times. They feel good about themselves so they don't find their significance on the useless side of life. They have a sense of belonging and competency.

One of Rudolf Dreikurs' favorite quotes was: "A child needs encouragement like a plant needs water." I believe that in order to help our children to really grow and become competent, self-reliant, and responsible people, encouragement is a necessity!

Allowances

Many parent-educators, counselors, and parents believe it is appropriate to set up an allowance system whereby children get paid for the jobs they do. However, I believe jobs and allowances should be separated. Children need to get an allowance because they are part of the family and do chores for the same reason.

Paying children for the jobs they do undermines the goal of helping the child develop a sense of belonging and competence. There is a drastic difference between asking the child, "Why do you help your parents with chores?" and hearing "Because they pay me," or asking the child, "Why do you help your parents with chores?" and hearing, "Because they **need** me!" Allowances can help children become competent and skillful.

When parents use money to motivate children to do chores, they often have to set up elaborate evaluation systems to determine how much of the allowance will be allotted. If the chore is not done properly a certain percentage of the allowance is withheld. This whole process can be discouraging to all involved. If the chores aren't getting done or people are slacking off, these are issues that can be discussed at a family meeting for making plans. (Family meetings for making plans are discussed on page 10.)

A very successful businessman told me in a family counseling session, "John, you really ask us to put a lot of time and effort into this family meeting stuff, and I was thinking the other day, if I tried to run my business the way I do my family, I'd be bankrupt in a month." I agreed with his premise that we have planning meetings to set up routines and discuss problems in business, but with something as important as one's family, we sometimes don't put out the effort.

I recommend that children in a family don't all get the same allowances. Older children usually have more needs than the younger ones. As children get older, they can look forward to getting a "raise" in their allowance each year. I suggest we give the children a certain amount for every year older they are. For example: children would get 20¢ per year. A two year-old would get 2 x 20¢ or 40¢. The five year-old would get 5 x 20¢ or $1.00. You adjust the allowance to what you think the child needs. The allowances can be the last business at the family meeting—a little incentive to keep the children involved in the meeting process.

When there are large jobs to do that parents would probably pay someone else to tackle, the children could contract for these in order to make extra money for a special need, such as a new ball, a glove, a special toy or game. Our sons contracted with us to paint our house when they were 8, 11 and 13 years-old. There are still some telltale paint signs on the sidewalk, but generally speaking, they did a great job. The feeling of accomplishment was obvious. Replacing the fence, cleaning out gutters, washing the car, and many other jobs could also be contract jobs.

Many parents train their children at a very early age to save some of their allowance in some kind of a savings account. "Chris, out of your $2.00 weekly allowance, do you want to put 30¢ or 40¢ into your savings?" asked one father.

There are many advantages to giving children allowances at a very young age. When you go to the store with the children and you get a whining request for money to buy candy, you need only reply, "That would be something you could spend your allowance on." Children can learn to save for something special and to understand that our every wish or desire is not instantly gratified. To learn to wait and save to get some things in this life is a positive outcome of this system.

When children break things intentionally or unintentionally, they can still pay for the damages with their allowances. You might have to set up a contract to pay back for something more expensive. For older children (ages 5 and up), I suggest interest be paid on the principal. Many lessons can be learned this way.

I suggested this method to foster parents who had a very destructive 13 year-old foster son living with them. He ran up a tremendous bill ($250.00) because he not only broke things, but he also stole from the parents. While they got upset with me because I couldn't come up with a better consequence, they stayed with my recommendation and after almost a year, the foster son broke even. He seldom behaved destructively after that.

A few years ago, I was counseling another family comprised of Mom, Dad and three year-old Samantha about the tremendous temper tantrums Samantha was throwing. We talked about starting an allowance and a Chore Chart for the three year-old. It was decided that Samantha would receive 60¢ a week which she divided into 20¢ for savings, 10¢ for church and 30¢ for frivolous spending.

Dad had recently refurbished a beautiful, old chest of drawers for Samantha. When she had her temper tantrums, Mom and Dad were now advised to go to their bedroom and not get caught up in a big fight with Samantha. When they first did this, Samantha was so enraged because they had changed their response to her temper tantrums that she took a toy truck and really "messed up" the beautiful dresser.

Dad was devastated, but rather than go into his typical rage, he waited until he was under control and then sat down with his daughter. He explained that he was hurt by what happened to the dresser, but he thought they (Dad and the daughter) needed to go the hardware store to purchase the necessary materials for repairing the chest.

"Out of the remaining 30¢ you have each week from your allowance, do you want to pay 15¢ or 20¢ for the repair materials?" Dad calmly asked.

Although she had a very little idea of the value of money, she chose 20¢. From then on (for at least three months) at every family meeting, Samantha got her 60¢ allowance and then divided it up with "20¢ for savings, 10¢ for church, and 20¢ for repair materials." The temper tantrums reduced significantly and Samantha was learning one of the most important lessons we can teach our children—the value of money.

Clothing Allowance

Again, when our children were 8, 11, and 13 years old respectively, a friend of ours, Perry Campbell, told us about clothing allowances. We only wish we had set up this system when the children were younger.

We calculated how much money we usually spent on the children's new clothes each year. We divided that into quarters so that each son got 25% of his clothing allowance every three months.

From then on, it was their responsibility to buy their own clothes. If they decided they wanted to buy one pair of jeans rather than two pairs from Mervyn's, that was their decision. While the whole "name brand" issue has become a "hot" topic for disagreement in some homes, our sons consulted with each other, watched for ads, and were satisfied to shop at discount clothing stores.

While there were certain restrictions we insisted on, such as not allowing the purchase of some tee-shirts that were totally inappropriate for people their age or probably any age, our sons did a very responsible job of purchasing their clothes. The most encouraging part of this system is that they wore the clothes they bought. Many times, this was not the case with the clothes we bought for them.

Communicating With Our Children

To be encouraging to our children, we must learn how to communicate more effectively with them. While there have been many books written about communication, parents often tell me that communication with their children is almost nonexistent. They try to talk with their children, especially teenagers, but parents never seem to be able to get anything out of them.

I always ask for an example of the parent's attempt to start a conversation with the child and it *always* goes like this.

"Hi, Chris, how was your day?" says Mom.

"Fine," Chris says, moving things around in the refrigerator.

"Well, what did you do?" asks Mom, taking a seat at the kitchen table.

"Nothing," says Chris, picking nuts off a chocolate cookie.

"What do you mean? Didn't you do anything down there at that school? Are you telling me you didn't do anything today? Every time I try to talk with you this is what happens," says an exasperated Mom.

One other question we *always* ask in a menacing tone of voice when the child comes home from school is, "Do you have any homework, dear?" This is a "deadly" question.

" No," says the child, "I just got hit by a Mac truck."

The parent will still respond with, "I don't care about that. Where is your homework?"

"The teacher didn't give us any," or "I finished it in class," or "I forgot it," are all possible answers from the child.

The parent gets very upset and says, "You always forget your homework" or "You got a 'D' on your last spelling test, so why don't you bring home your spelling book so you could work on it and do better in the future?"

Trying to start a conversation with our children by asking a question is definitely counter-productive. A close friend of mine, Lynn Lott, jokingly suggests that teenagers sometime become "psychoid" when we ask them the question, "How was school today?"

The teenager will almost always scream back, "What do you think? You think I wasn't in school? You think I was smoking dope? You never trust me!"

The questions don't sound like conversation-starters to the child. They sound like an _interrogation_. When we don't know someone too well, or we meet a stranger at a social event, we interview each other. "How are you, where do you work, are you married, do you have any children?" we ask. We generally start conversations by asking questions. But asking questions of our children is like extracting information and it is a definite communication stopper.

I suggest that parents attempt to start a conversation by making a statement about what they did during the day. For example, "Today, I saw a woman in the elevator at our office, and she had on this funny hat. It was so cute and she was such a nice person. Do you have anything you would like to tell me about your day?" The child may respond by telling the parent about his day, or he may not, but the probability of getting a conversation started is higher if you don't try to start out with a question.

Thomas Gordon in his book, _Teacher Effectiveness Training_, lists 12 roadblocks to communication. I find that the interrogation roadblock is one of the most effective in stopping communication not only between parent and child but between spouses or significant others.

Using "I" messages (as originally developed by Dr. Gordon) can help in communicating with each other and with our children. Using a "you" message is immediately heard as an attack. You can imagine your response to, "Why didn't _you_ feed the dog? _You_ make me so angry because _you_ never do what _you_ are told!"

The "I" message changes the focus of control from the child to the adult. We need to remember four steps or statements. These need to be memorized and practiced. I find it helpful to write down an "I" message before I say it, especially if this is a new idea. For example:

(1) When you _____

(2) I feel _____

(3) Because _____

(4) I would appreciate or I need you to _____

Possible answers include (1) when you don't come home at our agreed-on curfew, or when you don't do your chores; (2) I feel worried and scared, or I feel angry and taken for granted; (3) because I don't know where you are and so many bad things are happening nowadays on the streets, or because I work all day; and (4) I need you to call or come home on time, or I need your help just to make it through the day.

Many of my clients will say that this is not a natural way to talk to each other. I suggest it's not necessarily natural; it is the opposite of how we have **learned** to talk to each other. We need to take responsibility for our own feelings and thoughts rather than always blaming them on someone else. Dr. Rudolf Dreikurs suggested that blaming everyone else is a part of the slave mentality of our autocratic past, where "someone else" always made me do it. The king, the prince, the boss, the husband, and the priest were the authority figures that made people do things. We are becoming more and more aware that there is only one person who can make us do anything and that person, of course, is one's self.

Gary Golomb, a young man of 13, often begins conversations with his mother by asking, "If you had *one* wish today, Mom, what would it be?" The two of them make a point of asking each other this question each day. Mom will ask, "Hey, Gary, if you had one wish today, what would it be?" It helps them communicate exactly what they are feeling, as well as share information about their day.

Try using a statement about your day as a possible conversation starter rather than by asking questions. You may find it very, very difficult to do because we are all conditioned to start a conversation by asking, "How are you doing?" or "Did you have a good day?" or

"What's happening?" You may find you get a much better response from your child when you stop the "interrogation process."

Family Meeting

Many articles and even books have been written about family meetings. (See Additional Reading sources at the end of this book for references on Family Meetings). The main objectives of the family meeting are to work toward a cooperative atmosphere in the home and give all family members a feeling of belonging—and, thus, encouragement.

I'd like to share some suggestions I make to parents when they are trying to initiate family meetings. Parents often use the family meeting as another forum for telling the children what to do. This is usually a good reason why the meetings don't work out.

It is important to begin the family meeting with participants making encouraging statements to each other. This helps to create a positive atmosphere for problem solving. Everyone can make one positive statement about each family member.

The first attempt at a meeting should be limited to making a plan for when and how long subsequent meetings should be. The meeting should be done weekly and should not be put "on hold" unless something very serious interrupts the schedule. For some children, especially older ones, talking about having a "Planning Meeting" rather than a "Family Meeting" is sometimes helpful. Getting everyone's schedule together and making a plan for making it through the week is a good way to start. Who takes whom to soccer games or music lessons, who is going to cook, and getting the Chore Chart set up can all be planning issues for the first few meetings.

As a more cooperative atmosphere begins to develop, problems can be discussed. The first few meetings should be led by the parents as these are training sessions in cooperation. After that, the leadership rotates. An old friend gave us a gavel he brought home from Europe. That became the symbol of leadership at our family meetings.

A note taker is important to keep track of what has been accomplished as a result of having the meetings. Obviously, the parent needs to do this until the children become more competent, and then this job rotates also.

When a problem is discussed and consequences have been listed, it is best to get a consensus from the group on which one will be helpful. If a consensus is not forthcoming, I think it is very constructive to go to a vote, with the majority decision as the accepted consequence. It doesn't hurt children and adults to learn that we can have differences of opinions and still live together in a cooperative atmosphere.

Having an agenda for the meeting is helpful in getting parents out of the middle of some of the children's fights. When one of the children comes to tattle that "sister took my book out of my room," the parent can empathetically respond with, "That sounds like a good item to put on the agenda. It's over on the refrigerator. We will talk about it at our next meeting." Often, just putting an item on the agenda is all the child needs to do. When the item comes up at the meeting, the children or parents often say, "Oh, we already worked that out," or, "That's no longer a concern." It is helpful to prioritize items and then put a time limit on each.

The process of working through the family meeting is just as, or more important, than the product (solving family problems). In all the years we had our family meetings, we never did fully solve "pee on the toilet seats." With four males in the family, this was a frequent agenda item for Ann. We put signs up. We put targets in the toilet, and we put springs on the seats, but we were never entirely able to solve the problem. The process of working together to try to solve problems is important!

It is vital not to be too ambitious on "how all the problems will be solved" after the first meeting. Social problem solving is one of the most difficult jobs we have as human beings. It takes time for all of us to learn the give and take of living in a democratic home.

One of Rudolf Dreikurs' favorite quotes was "the only way to solve problems in a democratic society is through more democracy." This certainly holds true when working with family meetings.

Questions

1) How do children see the reward that is "handed down" from adult to child? p. 85

2) What do some children learn to do in order to be rewarded? p. 86

3) What is the author's definition of "encouragement"? p. 87

4) What is the first step we need to take to become more encouraging to our children? p. 88

5) Why can "feeling sorry" for a child be discouraging? pp. 88 - 89

6) Of the ten discouraging behaviors listed by parents, which rank high on your list? pp. 88 - 89

7) Are there other ways we discourage? Name a few.

8) Name some important phrases we can use in order to be encouraging? p. 89

9) What is a common pitfall for parents who are trying to encourage a discouraged, perfectionistic child? p. 91

10) According to the chart on p. 90, what is a helpful rule-of-thumb to determine if a statement is encouraging? p. 90

11) What are the major differences between praise/reward and encouragement as described in the chart on p. 90?

12) What should be the goal for any individual's or team's performance? p. 92

13) How can staying out of children's fights be encouraging? pp. 92 -93

14) What two suggestions are important to keep in mind when writing a letter of encouragement? p. 93

15) What does the author mean when he says encouraging children is a form of discipline? p. 94

16) According to the author, why should the allowance and payment for jobs be separate? pp. 94 - 95

17) What is the formula for setting up allowances that take the children's ages into account? p. 95

18) What are some advantages in giving out allowances at a young age? p. 96

19) What are the usual first two questions parents ask children when they come home from school? p. 98

20) Why does asking questions hinder communication? p. 99

21) What are the four statements we need to use with an "I" statement? p. 100 Give an example.

22) What are the main objectives of the family meeting? p. 101

23) How should the meeting begin? p. 101

24) Why is it helpful to have an agenda? p. 102

25) What was Dreikurs' idea about solving problems in a democratic society? p. 102

ACKNOWLEDGEMENTS

When one waits 53 years to write his first book, the acknowledgements could be endless.

This book is based on the philosophy and teachings of Rudolf Dreikurs and his teacher, Alfred Adler. Both my wife, Ann, and I were fortunate to have spent six summers studying with Dr. Dreikurs when he and his wife, Tee, taught at the University of Oregon and Oregon State University.

Gordon, our oldest son, had just been born when I took my first course from Dr. Dreikurs. His ideas and the Adlerian philosophy had a profound effect on our lives. We definitely used his ideas and techniques in raising our three sons: Gordon 30, Jeff 28, and David 25. As husbands, a father, a teacher, and as human beings, Ann and I could not be more proud of our sons. It is exciting to watch Gordon and his wife, Julie, use many of the same ideas in raising their daughters, Lee Anna and Sara. Jeff and his wife, Karen, both teachers, use many of the ideas and techniques in their classrooms. They are both considered excellent teachers by their administrators. David has also been able to apply many of Adler's and Dreikers' ideas in working very effectively with discouraged children.

I found Dreikurs' ideas were helpful to me in being a successful teacher and high school wrestling coach. Teams that I coached won two Oregon State Wrestling Championships, and placed Second, Third and Fourth between 1959 and 1968 by using a cooperative philosophy in the competitive field of wrestling.

Dreikurs' ideas influenced both Ann and me professionally as we are both in the counseling field. Ann is a very effective continuation high school counselor and I have a full private practice in marriage and family counseling.

Some of the best parent education I had was from my mother and father. My father was a very gentle person who had no macho problems with doing typical chores around the house. He definitely was a positive role model in my life. Mom used logical consequences and encouragement naturally (as you will see in the book). Although many children today can get "one up" on their parents, I never really was successful in doing that. My mother was always too smart for John Murray's challenges. We had chores in the home which I feel gave us a sense of belonging.

Two teachers and friends I feel taught me a lot about psychology and living are Dr. Dale Thomas, ageless wrestling coach and philosopher at Oregon State University and Dr. Oscar Christensen, my major professor at the University of Arizona. From them, I learned a great deal about mutual respect and encouragement.

Dr. Don Larson, resigned Assistant Superintendent of schools, and Mr. Glen Houde, retired Superintendent of Schools in Elk Grove, California gave Ann and me tremendous opportunities to develop parent-teacher education programs. Many of the experiences and anecdotes in the book came from 15 great years of working with these people.

My own family experiences have always influenced my outlook on how families can work together. Charlie, my older brother, has consistently been supportive and interested in me and what I do. He definitely encouraged me to write this book. My sister Cynthia, has been involved in parenting groups for years. She almost single-handedly started Adlerian study groups and training programs in her communities.

I can't say enough about Ann's encouragement and helpful support throughout our 31-year marriage. We worked together as a team and enjoyed raising our three sons. Although we didn't always agree on the "right way" to deal with certain child-rearing difficulties, we had a basic action plan that I think helped us get through some times that were difficult.

I also want to express my appreciation to my editor Gail Golomb. Without her pushing me to make an appointment with Grant Gibbs and Audrey Scannell of GraphicMasters, this book would never have gone to press.

Additional Reading

This list includes additional reading material on the subjects covered in the book. They are all highly recognized books and provide additional expert advice.

Adler, Alfred. *What Life Should Mean to You.* New York: G.P. Putnam's Sons, 1958.

Bettner, Betty Lou and Amy Lew. *Raising Kids Who Can.* Newton Center, Maine Connexions Press. 1990

Corsini, R.J., and G. Painter.*The Practical Parent.* New York: Harper & Row, 1975.

Dinkmeyer, D., and Rudolf Dreikurs. *Encouraging Children to Learn: The Encouragement Process.* Englewood Cliffs, N.J.: Prentice-Hall, 1963.

Dreikurs, Rudolph. *Social Equality: The Challenge of Today.* Chicago: Contemporary Books, Inc. 1971.

Dreikurs, R., S. Gould, and R.J. Corsini, *Family Council.* Chicago: Hinery Regnery Company, 1974.

Dreikurs, Rudolph, and L. Grey. *A New Approach to Discipline: Logical Consequences.* New York: Hawthorn Books, Inc., 1968.

Dreikurs, Rudolph, B. Grunwald, and F. Pepper. *Maintaining Sanity in the Classroom.* New York: Harper & Row, Inc., 1971.

Dreikurs, Rudolph, and V. Soltz. *Children: The Challenge.* New York: Hawthorn Books, Inc., 1964.

Forer, Lucille. *The Birth Order Factor.* New York: McKay, 1976.

Lansky, V. *101 Ways to Tell Your Child "I Love You."* Chicago, New York:Contemporary Books, 1988.

Nelson, J. *Positive Discipline.* New York. Ballantine Books, 1987.

Schnebly, L. *Out of Apples.* Tucson: Manzanita Press, 1987.

Thomas, Dr. Gordon. *TET: Teacher Effectiveness Training,* New York: Peter H. Wyden Publishing, 1974

APPENDIX

The following is a list of responsibilities that children at different ages of development are usually capable of doing. This list is only to stimulate your parental creativity in choosing even more possible jobs for your children.

2 Year Olds or Younger

1. Pick up unused toys and put in the proper place.
2. Put books and magazines in a rack.
3. Sweep the floor with small broom
4. Place napkins and silverware on or at the table. At first, the child might bring the table setting from the kitchen and place it on the chairs at the table. When the rest of the family comes for the meal, they pick up their place settings, put them on the table and sit down to eat.
5. Clean up what they spill or drop.
6. Make choices. What two foods for breakfast? What color sweater to wear? Which chair to sit in — (see limited chores section).
7. Clear the table of **plastic** dishes. Parents can put a dishpan on a very low stool where the 2 year old can stack the plates when she brings them to the kitchen.
8. If you have a **dishwasher**, the 2 year old can **help** load and unload.
9. Toilet training.
10. Simple hygiene – brush teeth, wash and dry hands, face, and brush hair.
11. Undress self and dress self with some help.
12. Carry boxed or canned goods from the grocery sacks to the proper shelf. Put some things away on a lower shelf.
13. Put weeds in a sack to assist the person who is pulling weeds.

4 Year Olds

1. Put place setting on the table while setting the table – with good dishes.

2. Put the groceries away.
3. Help with compiling a grocery list and with shopping.
4. Polish shoes and clean up afterwards.
5. Follow a schedule for feeding pets.
6. Help do yard and garden work.
7. Help make the beds and vacuum.
8. Help do the dishes or fill the dishwasher by themselves.
9. Dust the furniture.
10. Make lunches for school or work.
11. Prepare cold cereal.
12. Help mother prepare plates of food for the family dinner.
13. Make a salad.
14. Make a simple dessert (add topping to cupcakes, Jello, pour the toppings on ice cream).
15. Hold the hand mixer to whip potatoes or mix up a cake.
16. Share toys with friends.
17. Get the mail.
18. Tell parent his whereabouts before going out to play.
19. Be able to play without constant adult supervision and attention.
20. Bring milk from the refrigerator to the dinner table.
21. Hang socks, handkerchiefs, and washclothes on a lower line.
22. Polish silver.
23. Polish car.
24. Sharpen pencils.

5 Year-Olds

1. Help with the meal planning and grocery shopping.
2. Make simple breakfast and clean up.
3. Pour own drink.
4. Prepare the dinner table.
5. Add certain ingredients to a recipe.
6. Make bed and clean room.
7. Dress on own and choose outfit for the day (with two choices).
8. Clean mirrors and windows.

9. Separate clothing for washing, putting white clothes in one pile and colored in another.
10. Fold clean clothes and put them away.
11. Answer the telephone and begin to dial the phone for use.
12. Do yard work.
13. Pay for small purchases.
14. Help clean out the car.
15. Take out the garbage.
16. Decide how to spend his share of the family entertainment fund.
17. Feed his pets and clean their living area.
18. Learn to tie shoes.
19. Run own bathwater.

6 Year Olds

1. Choose own clothing for the day according to the weather or a special event.
2. Shake rugs.
3. Water plants and flowers.
4. Peel vegetables.
5. Cook simple food (boil egg and make toast).
6. Help hang clothes on the clothesline.
7. Hang up own clothes in the closet.
8. Gather wood for the fireplace.
9. Rake leaves and weeds.
10. Take dog for walk.
11. Tie own shoes.
12. Be responsible for own minor injuries.
13. Keep the garbage container clean.
14. Clean out inside of car.
15. Straighten or clean out silverware drawer.
16. Straighten or clean family library.
17. Help clean garage.

7 Year Olds

1. Oil and take care of bike and lock it when unused.
2. Take phone messages and write them down.
3. Run errands for parents.
4. Sweep and wash patio area.
5. Water the lawn.
6. Care for bike and other outside toys or equipment.
7. Wash dog or cat.
8. Train pets.
9. Carry in the grocery sacks.
10. Get self up in the morning and to bed at night on own.
11. Carry own lunch money and notes back to the school.
12. Leave the bathroom in order; hang up clean towels.
13. Do simple ironing; flat pieces.
14. Wash down walls and scrub floors.

8 and 9 Year Olds

1. Fold napkins properly and set silverware properly.
2. Mop or buff the floor.
3. Clean venetian blinds.
4. Help rearrange furniture. Help plan the layout.
5. Help others with their work when asked.
6. Straighten own closet and drawers.
7. Shop for and select own clothing and shoes, with parent.
8. Change school clothes without being told.
9. Fold blankets.
10. Sew buttons.
11. Sew rips in seams.
12. Clean storage room.
13. Clean up animal "messes" in the yard and house.
14. Begin to read recipes and cook for the family.
15. Babysit for short periods of time.
16. Cut flowers and make a center piece.
17. Pick fruit off trees.
18. Build a campfire, get items ready for "cook out" or barbeque.

19. Paint fence or shelves.
20. Help write simple letters.
21. Write thank you notes.
22. Help with defrosting and cleaning of the refrigerator.
23. Feed the baby.
24. Bathe younger sister or brother.
25. Polish silverware, copper or brass items.
26. Clean patio furniture.
27. "Endust" furniture.

9 and 10 Year-Olds
1. Change sheets on the bed and put dirty sheets in the hamper.
2. Operate the washer and/or the dryer.
3. Measure detergent and bleach.
4. Buy groceries using a list and do comparative shopping.
5. Cross streets unassisted.
6. Keep own appointments (dentist, school, etc., and have these appointments be within bike distance).
7. Prepare pastries from box mixes.
8. Prepare family meals.
9. Receive and answer own mail.
10. Make and pour tea, coffee and juices.
11. Wait on guests.
12. Plan birthday parties for others.
13. Use simple first aid.
14. Do chores for neighbors.
15. Sew, knit or weave.
16. Learn to use sewing machine.
17. Do chores without a reminder.
18. Learn about banking.
19. Wash the family car.

10 and 11 Year-Olds
1. Earn own money by babysitting, collecting and recycling aluminum cans and newspapers.

2. Be alone at home
3. Handle sums of money up to $5.00.
4. Be able to take the city bus.
5. When staying overnight with a friend, pack own suitcase.
6. Responsible for personal hobby.
7. Handle self properly when in public places alone or with peers (movie).

11 and 12 Year Olds

1. Join outside organizations, do assignments and attend functions.. Take responsibility as a leader.
2. Put siblings to bed and help dress them.
3. Clean pool and pool area.
4. Respect others' property.
5. Run own errands.
6. Mow lawn.
7. Help a parent build things and assist with the family errands.
8. Clean oven and stove.
9. Schedule self ample time for studies.
10. Be responsible for a paper route.
11. Check and add oil to car if necessary.

It is the author's hope you have benefitted from reading this book. If you are interested in purchasing additional copies, contact:

Dynamic Training and Seminars, Inc.
Publishing Division
8902 Quartzite Circle
Roseville, CA 95661
or call
1-800-262-4387

Please include a check or money order for $10.00 plus $2.00 for postage and handling. California residents kindly include sales tax.